GLOBE POLITICS

NAVEED QAZI

ISBN 13: 9798370822148

Formatting, proofreading and editing done by the author.

Typeset in Adobe Caslon Pro
Cover design also by Naveed Qazi.
www.naveedqazi.com

CONTENTS

ABBREVIATIONS

AFRC Armed Forces Revolutionary Council
AWACS Airborne Warning and Control Systems
ASEAN Association of Southeast Asian Nations
AU African Union
AQAP Al Qaeda in Arabian Peninsula
AIP Islamic Party of Azerbaijan
BBC British Broadcasting Corporation
BN *Barisan Nasional (Malay)*
CIA Central Intelligence Agency
CV Curriculum Vitae
CNN Cable News Network
CPEC China Pakistan Economic Corridor
EU European Union
ECOWAS Economic Community of West African States
FALCON Flag Alcatel Lucent Optimal Network
GDP Gross Domestic Product
GME Maghreb Europe Gas Pipeline
GCC Gulf Cooperation Council
HD Centre for Humanitarian Dialogue
ISIS Islamic State of Iraq and Syria
IRA Irish Republican Army
IRGC Islamic Revolutionary Guard Corps
JCPOA Joint Comprehensive Plan of Action
KCK *Koma Civaken Kurdistanê (Kurdish)*
LGBT Lesbian, Gay, Bisexual, Transgender
LSE London School of Economics
MSNBC Microsoft National Broadcasting Company
MAK Movement for Self-determination of Kabylie
MAD Mutually Assured Destruction
MFDC Movement of Democratic Forces in Casamance
MPSR *Movement Patriotique Pour La Sauvegarde Et La*

Restauration (French)
MSF *Médecins Sans Frontieres (French)*
MQM *Muttahida Qaumi Movement (Urdu)*
MPP Migration Protection Protocol
MP Member Parliament
NATO North Atlantic Treaty Organisation
NGO Non-Governmental Organisation
NPRC National Peace and Reconciliation Commission
OSCE Organisation for Security and Co-operation in Europe
OUN-B Organisation of Ukrainian Nationalists (Bandera)
OIC Organisation of Islamic Countries
PAS *Party Islam Se Malaysia (Malay)*
PJD Justice and Development Party
PKK *Partiya Karkeren Kurdistan (Kurdish)*
PTI *Pakistan Tehreek-e-Insaf (Urdu)*
PPP Pakistan People's Party
PML-N Pakistan Muslim League-Nawaz
PMF Popular Mobilisation Forces
PH *Pakatan Harapan (Malay)*
R2P Responsibility to Protect
RNI National Rally of Independents (Morocco)
RSF Reporters Without Borders
RSF Rapid Support Forces
SANA Syrian Arab News Agency
SADR Sahrawi Arab Democratic Republic
SLPP Sierra Leone Peoples Party
SWIFT Society for Worldwide Interbank Financial Telecommunications
SDF Syrian Democratic Forces
SVT Sveriges Television
TIMEP Tahrir Institute for Middle East Policy
TV Television
UAV Unmanned Aerial Vehicles
UAE United Arab Emirates

US United States
UK United Kingdom
UN United Nations
YPG *Yekineyen Parastina Gel (Kurdish)*

1

BELARUS BECOMING A PASSAGE FOR MIGRANTS TO EUROPE

When Alexander Lukashenko crushed a nationwide revolt against his fraudulent presidential victory, he had been hampered by sanctions since the summer of 2020 by the United States, and the European Union which were biting hard. In response, Lukashenko began offering a safe passage for Middle Easterners to Europe, first to Minsk, the capital of Belarus, and then, often by government bus, to Poland, Lithuania, and Latvia. The motive behind his act was to force the EU to ease its sanctions against Belarus, by directly threatening an immigration flood tide. In some cases, migrants had even paid five to ten thousand dollars to come to Belarus, reflecting money profiteering by Lukashenko's regime. However, there were also others, mostly economic migrants, who had come with some minimal expense.

The desperation was summed up right by Dexter Fillins in his The New Yorker essay, who wrote: 'Whatever else Lukashenka's scheme is, it's ingenious: the broken countries of the Middle East and Central Asia are filled with young men and women looking for better lives, and the doors to Europe are otherwise locked tight.'

Lukashenko had publicly denied that he was enabling immigrants to flow into Europe, but his denials are not creditworthy, especially when Iraqi migrants in Poland have been testifying to the fact that they had been given wire cutters by Belarusian security forces.

Lukashenko is not the first national leader to use the threat of unrestrained immigration for political purposes. Just like Lukashenko, Erdogan has also threatened to allow free passage for the Syrian refugees inside his country, who number 3.6 million. The EU had responded to his move with large tranches of financial aid to help him pay for the immigrants, showing that Erdogan is making Europe to dance on his tunes.

Artyom Shraibman, a political analyst based in Minsk and a non-resident scholar at the Carnegie Endowment for International Peace's Moscow Center believes that Lukashenko has threatened to open his borders, long ago, before the political crises of 2020, but his threats increased since 2021.

To stop the migrants, the governments of Lithuania, Latvia, and Poland have deployed troops to their borders with Belarus, and they have deported most of those who have made it across. Other measures, such as the construction of migrant camps, are expensive, and they remain a matter at hand.

Under pressure from the European Union, Belavia in November 2021 had stopped allowing Iraqis, Syrians, and Yemenis, to board flights in Turkey, and the Turkish government, in retaliation, said that it would stop selling tickets to Belarus. But, Belavia flies throughout the Middle East and Central Asia.

These regions have droves of eager young people who want to go to Europe. And, according to Landsbergis, Lithuanian foreign minister, thousands of Iraqis, Afghans, and Kurds have already arrived in Belarus, waiting to cross.

When the migrants approach the border of any one of

the EU states, they are pushed back. At the same time, the government of Belarus does not want them, either. That is why, thousands of migrants appear to be stuck in what is literally a no man's land, a hell hole. They are living in freezing camps, in forests with no humanitarian aid. Many of them have died. Migrants who were dead left traces such as food wrappers, former makeshift campsites, paperwork in Arabic, and even boarding passes from their home countries.

Belarus was later accused of employing migrants as a form of hybrid warfare against the European Union after Latvia, Lithuania, and Poland declared a state of emergency. Some of these countries also institutionalised riot policing, and other measures to bolster the border guards.

The right-wing governing party in Poland has long called non-European migrants a threat to Polish culture and sovereignty, and its response to the current situation has been predictably heated. This stance is something similar that buoyed the right-wing nationalists across the continent.

Under pressure from the European Union, which does not want an encore of the 2015 migrant crises only some migrants from the border were shifted to some warehouses and some to government-run hotels by Belarus, where they were provided with some basic assistance.

The other point to note is that as most of them are economic migrants, they do not qualify for asylum, heightening their fears of survival. People who tried to help the migrants have had their cars smashed.

Also, the key to this migrant crisis has been Putin. He has been Lukashenko's benefactor and guarantor. For years, the Russian government has provided Lukashenko with billions of dollars' worth of subsidised gas and oil, which it can sell at market prices elsewhere. These subsidised fuels are pivotal in sustaining Moscow's satrapy in Minsk. In 2020, during the popular uprising against Lukashenko, Putin made it clear that he would, if necessary, use force to keep Belarus from slipping out of Russian hands. In this view, the immigration crisis unfolding in Europe is a battle between Russia and the West, which puts Belarus at its very centre. And, in this battle, it is not just Belarus.

There are other former states of the Soviet Union that have become hotbeds of East-West competition too. Add to that, in Belarus, Ukraine, Georgia, and Moldova, there are overwhelming popular aspirations to move closer to Europe, making these stances palpable against the hard calculations of Russian power.

Lukashenka will not hold on to Belarus forever, but, as the events mainly on the Polish and Lithuanian borders continue to unfold, he may have invented a weapon that will tow with us for a long time to come.

January 15, 2022

2

GUINEAN COUP YET ANOTHER NORMAL IN TURBULENT AFRICA

Colonel Mamady Doumbouya became Guinea's interim president in September 2021 after leading a coup against Alpha Conde. The ex-president had once put faith in the colonel to keep his grip on the turbulent nation-state. But, according to Doumbouya, who mostly keeps a low profile, Conde was a man with two faces. The former French legionnaire believed that the army had little choice but to seize power because of his rampant corruption, disregard for human rights and economic mismanagement. That is why, he went out on TV, wearing a red beret, sunglasses, and an army fatigue, announcing a takeover. The junta had made plans for a transitional rule, but they did not specify how long will it take the transition to take form. They are also adamant to release Conde, only if he publicly resigns.

The military's frustration in instigating the coup shows that the world had turned a blind eye to Conde's abuses. That is why after the coup, the colonel commented: 'If the people are crushed by their elites, it is up to the army to give the people their freedom.' It led many euphoric Guineans to the streets in celebration.

What Conde did by making constitutional changes, was like what his predecessor had done: the dictator Lansana Conte had fought so hard not to depose, by staying in power for two decades.

After he died in 2008, there was a coup, by Captain Moussa Dadis Camara, which saw rapes of dozens of women, and over one hundred fifty people were killed, as a reaction.

It eventually made Conde come into power. After becoming the president, Conde was seen as a relentless crusader, for democracy and human rights, and a foe of corruption. He made the right economic policies, by efficiently utilising the mining and bauxite resources, which set a certain social contract with the Guineans, who re-elected him in 2015. However, he then squandered it all, and his lust for power resulted in an axe on his toe.

Apart from Guinea, attempts at the third term had been done recently by President Alassane Ouattara in Ivory Coast in 2020, Blaise Compaore in Burkina Faso in 2014, and Niger's President Mamadou Tandja in 2010. There even have been recent other coups in Mali, Chad, and Sudan.

Conde's years also saw increasing ethnicisation of Guinean politics, notably between Diallo's Fulani group and Conde's Malinke, which together account for some seventy per cent of the population.

Rivalries within the military sections also did not help. Conde and his defence minister established a parallel elite force, clearly designed to crush the growing prominence of Doumbouya's forces.

International organisations did not take the coup lightly though. They greeted the colonel with scorn: the African Union suspended Guinea, two days after the ECOWAS did the same. The United Nations, European Union, United States, and France have all condemned the coup and called for Conde's release.

Commoners, however, had seen the colonel, who led the coup, as a man with a strong physique, and character, who charismatically led the parades. Many wanted to take photographs with him and cheered for him. Although, there is a section that believes that his credentials are dubious.

Apart from that, military coups, almost every time, result in a more brutal system of governance, than the ones they replace. For the military, what would also become problematic is their isolation from international financial institutions and the international community, which may force the junta to form an interim civilian government.

When it comes to the political opposition, they, interestingly, celebrated the coup, too. Prominent civil society and opposition leaders, notably Cellou Dalein Diallo, who lost the 2020 presidential election to Conde called the coup 'a necessary evil' to reverse the country's descent into autocracy.

The coup leaders seem to be saying and doing all the right things so far. Political prisoners have been released, and the main opposition party has been allowed to access its headquarters, after it being blocked for months by Conde's regime.

West African political analyst Paul Melly is of an opinion that Colonel Doumbouya has a certain advantage in ruling the country, post-coup, as he has done international assignments related to peacekeeping missions and some international interventions. Also, he has done military training in France and has experience in over eight countries.

After Conde toyed with the constitution, the military, post-coup, had insisted on a new charter as well, which claims to be 'free, transparent and democratic.'

What has happened in Guinea, reflects that the days of coups are not yet over in Africa. They first happened during the post-independence era. It even involved counter coups and failed coups. African political history also shows that as its leaders banned opposition parties, the alteration of power became only possible through the barrel of the gun. Between 1960 and 2000, the overall number of coups and coup attempts stood at an average of four per year, according to a study by Jonathan Powell, an associate professor at the University of Central Florida, and Clayton Thyne, a professor at the University of Kentucky.

Analysts believe that the recent surge in militarisation in politics is driven by external forces, including many actors, who want to prioritise their interests in Africa, and internal factors such as public venting against corruption, insecurity, and poor governance.

African Union and ECOWAS also largely lack credibility in Guinea, which supplies crucial aluminium stock to Russian and Chinese industries, reflecting massive industrial commitments.

They are also seen as a 'big men club,' protecting insiders, showing a need for a change in thinking in their policy, which may involve wider discussions with several Guinean social and political groups, their leaders, recognition of ethnic lines, and respecting the mass sentiment.

They have also not slapped any sanctions yet, or defined any invasions, hinting at a softer approach.

At the same time, they seem to be in a difficult position right now to negotiate with the coup leaders.

January 17, 2022

3

GRAVITY OF POLITICAL SITUATION IN KAZAKHSTAN

The protests in the oil-rich Kazakhstan gained momentum in January 2022, when a crumbling old town in western Kazakhstan called Zhanaozen stirred in protests, as security forces killed some workers, who had gone to strike over late pay checks, and poor living conditions. The sudden gas price hike has also been seen as an economic failure to ensure security for its people. However, it remains a mystery how from a grimy, Soviet-era settlement near the Caspian Sea protests suddenly spread across thousand miles, even turning Almaty, its largest city, into a war zone, littered with dead bodies, burned buildings including the mayor's office, and incinerated cars. It shocked everyone, including its leader, who fortified Almaty with Russian troops. By ordering to fire without warning, to restore order, government critics have long bridled at government oppression and rampant corruption in the oil-rich nation.

After the protests gained momentum, especially after the statue of Nursultan Nazarbayev was brought down, Kazakhstan was sealed off from the world. Its airports were closed and commandeered by Russian troops, and information to collect became scarce, as phone and Internet services were barred.

Echoing the repressive idioms, President Kassym-Jomart Tokayev even lashed out at liberals and human rights defenders, lamenting that the authorities had been too lax when they were not, as they detained thousands of people. The president claimed that the recent uprising was the work of some twenty thousand bandits, who he believed were commanded from a single post. Pacifying with them, according to him, was sheer stupidity, and he just wanted them to be 'destroyed.' It all reflected the gravity of the situation.

The slogan of the protests was *Shal, ket!* ('Old man, leave!'), a not-so-polite invitation to the 81-year-old Nazarbayev to forgo power. The demonstrations and riots shook the regime that the patriarch, in his reigning political past, had built and fortified for over more than three decades. Galym Ageleulov, a human-rights activist in Almaty who took part in the demonstrations believed that what began initially as a peaceful demonstration suddenly turned into mob violence, and people who did it were not students, bookish dissidents and middle-class malcontents, a sort of class who usually turn out for protests in Kazakhstan.

Among those who urged the crowd to vehemency was Arman Dzhumageldiev, known as 'Arman the Wild,' one of the country's most powerful crime bosses, who witnesses believe provoked much of the violence. He gave frantic speeches on Almaty's central square as government buildings blazed behind him, calling for people to press the government to make concessions. It ultimately led the interior ministry to his arrest. Firearms and edged weapons, military body armour and an armoured car were seized from him.

Danil Kislov, a Russian expert on Central Asia who runs Fergana, a news portal focused on the region, speculated that the chaos was the result of a desperate struggle for power between feuding political clans, namely people loyal to Tokayev, and those beholden to his 81-year-old predecessor, Nursultan Nazarbayev. But there seems to be more to it, than mere palace intrigues, as rising social inequality among Kazakhs is also something that needs to be considered.

In the recent past, many Kazakhs have derided the system created by Nazarbayev as deeply corrupt and unjust. His family members and clique became some of the most powerful people in Kazakhstan, occupying top public positions. They also ranked among the richest people on the planet, living lives of extravagance. Corruption hollowed out governance, with civil servants rewarded for their loyalty rather than their acumen. All this even put constant pressure on independent media, and human rights groups were also eventually marginalised.

Rivalries have simmered inside the family court, and they have occasionally come into public view. In 2001, Nazarbayev's son-in-law Rakhat Aliyev was removed from his position as the powerful chair of the National Security Committee, after allegedly plotting a coup. In fact, authorities have accused four different chairs of this committee, including Nazarbayev's ally Karim Massimov in the wake of the recent tumult.

When it comes to the question of Russian military intervention, it even irked the United States, and they wanted to understand the situation better. On the recent Kazakh conundrum, Secretary of State, Antony Blinken said: 'One lesson in recent history is that once Russians are in your house, it's sometimes very difficult to get them to leave.'

The fragility of Kazakh politics can be measured by reflecting upon how quickly a possible power struggle morphed into the mayhem on the streets. It also shows how brittle Kazakhstan is, beneath the shiny surface of wealthy, cosmopolitan cities like Almaty. The country is now becoming as repressive as most in a region dominated by brutal strongmen: the former dictator of neighbouring Uzbekistan, Islam Karimov, was accused of boiling his critics in vats of oil and having hundreds of protesters massacred in the town of Andijan in 2005. Kazakhstan's political development is stunted by twenty years of authoritarian rule, and the citizens are still having a cold shoulder about the kleptocratic elite who instead of listening to their everyday problems, preferred to pour billions of dollars into the construction of a new city, named Nursultan, in the honour of the former president.

In fact, this kind of discontent has happened before. When police killed at least fourteen people (and maybe dozens more) in Zhanaozen during an oil workers' strike in 2011, that tragic event was the biggest blot in the history of independent Kazakhstan, until the new protests emerged in 2022.

Kazakhstan has traditionally balanced ties with Russia, China, and the West. For Russia, the operation provided an opportunity to expand its influence in Kazakhstan and in the region. The operation also has strengthened Russia's hand going into talks with the United States on Ukraine.

According to an Op-ed in Foreign Affairs by Nargis Kassenova, Tokayev has eventually insisted on the direction of socioeconomic reforms, after the recent unrest. They seem to be already well-defined. Tokayev wants to build a modern welfare state. In his address to the parliament on January 11, 2022, he acknowledged the problematic distribution of wealth in Kazakhstan, and how the benefits of economic growth have fallen to a narrow class.

He criticised government agencies for hardship in Kazakhstan, masking 'the real situation with terms like productive self-employed, informal employment' and leaving many people 'in a state of unemployment and social insecurity.' He called for a 'qualitative renewal of social and labour policies.' These reforms suggest that Tokayev has now been paying attention to the demands of the street. It also reflects a growing international trend that is away from free-market economics and tilts towards improved social welfare protections.

Optimists hope that Tokayev will expunge the most abominable elements of the Nazarbayev era. Nevertheless, the political system remains fundamentally the same. Tokayev has, in the past, signalled that he wants to improve channels of communication and trust between the state and the people, but such rhetoric has so far proved to be indecisive

January 19, 2022

4

SINN FEIN STILL HAS A LOT OF GROUND TO COVER

There is a possibility that Sinn Fein, a political wing of an armed organisation, might become a party to the government in a European Union member state in the future, despite the fact the opinion polls show them popular in only more than a quarter of the Irish public. It calls for a united Ireland and is more than an anti-establishment populist front. The party claims to reimagine itself as having an alternative vision for Irish people on both sides of the border.

The people's mood, despite its rise, is something different. It runs contrary to their unification and nationalist agenda, as per opinion polls done by the University of Liverpool Institute of Irish Studies, and Times Survey.

These facts are not news for Irish nationalists, either. They, for over a century, have predicted the demise of the absorption of Northern Ireland into the Republic. British Unionists are aware of this fact, and it gives them a chance to secure Northern Ireland into the United Kingdom even further. In a blog on politics.co.uk, Kevin Meagher analysed the priorities for Sinn Fein, and commented: 'Either Sinn Fein ends up as a coalition partner in government and actively promotes Irish unity, or it influences the political weather as the main opposition party.'

The gradual popularity, however, is making many analysts believe that Sinn Fein belongs to the same cadre of parties in Europe that became successful after their vitriolic protest movements. It included the Five Star Movement in Italy and Servant of the People in Ukraine.

The party, historically, had ties with Irish Republican Provos, and it had marred many Irish voters in the late 20th century. Although the current party framing of a 'United Ireland' stands as a goal by political means rather than violence, one cannot deny Sinn Fein's past associations with IRA extremism.

It was in February 2018, after more than thirty-four years at its helm, Irish politician Gerry Adams stepped down as the leader of Sinn Fein. In his place rose Mary Lou McDonald, who outlined her vision for the party in her first address, committing to 'innovative and modern ways of advancing Irish politics.'

Despite this, the rebranding of Sinn Fein has helped their nationalist messaging which carefully directs the language to foment a nationalism of unity over divisions, mainly the Catholic and Protestant fuss. McDonald's caucus campaigned on a United Ireland, based on the preservation of Irish culture, in terms of support for the colonised Irish Gaelic language. In doing so, the party appealed to the struggling white working-class voters including immigrants, who were also white. This fact can be vouchsafed by their good electoral performance in their respective territories.

To put brakes on their rise in the future, the other two parties namely Fine Gael and Fianna Fail are trying to make a grand coalition, and this development is trying to push Sinn Fein on the centre-right in orientation, which traditionally adheres to left-wing nationalism. If this happens, it will give, some dissenting voices within the

Fianna Fail, a hope of tie-up with Sinn Fein, as they see it as a good fit. The scenario, nevertheless, has also allowed a perfect left-right political orientation to emerge in Irish politics currently.

Since the 2016 Brexit referendum, there has been a rise in dissident republican activity in Northern Ireland, and the prospect of a hard border between the Republic and Northern Ireland has been a major contributor to the increase of recruits to the IRA as well. It is something alarming to British Unionism.

In its history, Sinn Fein splintered into several groups, most of whom claimed the old revolutionary party's title and legacy. However, it was the faction led by Gerry Adams, which toed the line between idealism and pragmatism. It would ultimately see success, as the party sat its first member of the southern Irish legislature in 1997, and quickly became the largest pro-reunification party in Northern Ireland, leading the call to reunite with the Republic of Ireland in the Northern Irish assembly.

The present vote share for Sinn Fein is also showing that it is going mainstream, much attributed to its popular leader, McDonalds, who is seen as a poised, fluent Dubliner, having a classless appeal among its supporters. The party is also ahead of other political parties, in terms of social media campaigning. The murder of Paul Quinn in 2007, alleged by its IRA supporters did not hinder its growing popularity. However, most of the population in Ireland is under 25, and memories of The Troubles remain secondary to them. It is something that will give a hard time to Sinn Fein to muster its nationalist electoral growth in the future.

As Sinn Fein has gone mainstream, and channels all its

energy, effort, politics, and social capital mostly on united Ireland, it may end up losing its vote share. Aidan Regan, associate professor at University College Dublin's school of politics, said in a podcast that Sinn Fein immediately should broaden its political objectives that include multiple issues plaguing the lives of common people and industry. Some of the things Sinn Fein tried to address are the collapsing housing market and tax reform. For a start, it had already called to build a hundred thousand homes, announced a three-year rent freeze, and greater transparency in tax, especially in the case of multinationals.

January 22, 2022

5

TRIUMPH OF THE TALIBAN

In August 2021, the Taliban swept the whole of Afghanistan in less than a week. The capture was an ominous one, and the most significant coup d'etat in the region. It all began when a Taliban commander won a fight with Afghan forces in the southwestern border capital of Zaranj.

Zaranj's fate then set a pattern, as Taliban insurgents overrun state defences in a continuous effort. Within a matter of days, other cities such as the key city of Kunduz in the north, Pul-e-Khumri and Ghazni, sitting on the strategic approaches to Kabul fell, too. Then, in the most devastating blow, the second and third largest cities of Kandahar and Herat would also fall to the Taliban.

Taliban's advance in 2021 has also brought stories of horror, including details of reprisals against former government workers, summary executions, beheadings, and kidnappings of girls for forced marriages. There were bodies lying in the prisons, with dogs next to them.

As the Taliban pressed their growing advantage, ambassadors were trying to evacuate their embassies, as insurgents cut the main roads between cities, and started deals for the capitulation of state forces. The despondent, often hungry, defeated defenders started registering complaints about how reinforcements promised by the erstwhile civilian government in Kabul failed to arrive at many places.

Amid the advance, many commoners wanted to flee the country. They kept crowding at the gates of Kabul's parks, and other open spaces. Families were fighting for food. However, there was a specific class of people who also welcomed the Taliban, approaching their gun-toting occupiers for selfies.

After the sudden demise of the civilian government, politicians and analysts kept on wondering how all this happened, when Americans had funnelled trillions of dollars into Afghanistan's security forces, numbering about three hundred thousand, whose abilities were long touted by Western generals.

Ashraf Ghani's sudden departure, without informing anyone, also led to the collapse of police machinery and the army, and a vacuum was created which was difficult to fill.

The Taliban had adopted an emirate label for governance, and incorporated several new features in the government, including the 1964 constitution, which is a monarchist constitution. Since their triumph on the streets of Afghanistan, they formed an interim government without any hassle and were dictating terms.

They all along had wanted a council of senior clerics, like Iran's guardian council, to vet laws and decrees based on their conformity with religious law. Many of the ministries are now being run by college-educated Islamists.

Also, Ghani's perception to test their power on the battlefield in 2020 and 2021 was ill-judged. With the Taliban in power again, Afghanistan was even coined by people as the world's first narco-state.

For Ryan Crocker, who was the US ambassador to Afghanistan under Barack Obama, the answer to the Taliban's victory was straightforward. Biden's plan to continue with the withdrawal of US forces was akin to 'giving the country to Taliban fighters'. Other critical observers, such as the US special inspector general for Afghanistan reconstruction, which has tracked corruption and waste in the US-led effort, have put a warning note since long on whether the money spent on military training and salaries was well spent, cautioning that the 'question … will ultimately be answered by the outcome of the fighting on the ground'.

One of the other serious mistakes, the Afghan army did was defending the inner cities only, and not the countryside, letting the Taliban isolate and besiege provincial capitals, and cut off lines of communication, ultimately squeezing Kabul. Add to that, the Afghan army had low morale, for various intrinsic reasons, which included monetary, such as the prospect of a good salary. Taliban, on the other hand, invested heavily in religious education and cultural affinity, which gave them stronger reasons to fight to death and capture, despite being lightly armed.

Tribal elders were also seen negotiating a pullout. This important scenario reflected a defeat that was foretold and long coming. Bill Roggio, a senior fellow at the Foundation for Defence of Democracies, who has chronicled the war, echoed this assessment.

The rapidity of the Taliban's victory has delivered a tremendous boost to Islamists everywhere – be it Syria, Mozambique, jihadists sitting in Birmingham, Manila, or even Kashmir. When a breeding ground has been reborn, it has made many believe that al-Qaeda will soon have its political and military arsenal redeployed.

According to a UN assessment, al Qaeda is already present in fifteen per cent of Afghanistan, and al-Qaeda in the Indian subcontinent, an affiliate of the group, 'operates under Taliban protection from Kandahar, Helmand and Nimruz provinces.'

There has been a lack of coherence in understanding how Middle East politics shaped up when it came to recognising the power of extremist Islamist elements. Investigative journalist, Jason Burke went on to write in a Guardian Op-ed: 'one of the many reasons for the US failures in Afghanistan was an inability in the early years of the conflict there to distinguish between al-Qaeda, a small group of largely Arab Islamists committed to the overthrow of regimes in the Middle East as well as a war against Israel and the West, and the Taliban, a reactionary Afghan movement with a strong local ethnic and nationalist element that aimed to impose a rigorous religious rule on a single country.'

Relations between the Taliban, which contain many different factions, and al-Qaeda have evolved dramatically since. On occasions, they have been unpredictable, but most of the time cordial. As the decades have passed, personal relationships and familial links have been forged. Leaders of other militant networks have acted as intermediaries. Some priorities still differ. Although, the Taliban are very much more globally aware than they were twenty years ago. This makes them share the political worldview of al-Qaeda in new and important ways. US intelligence services, several times, have characterised the relationship as close.

After the takeover, the Taliban are trying to seek international legitimacy. It is a kind of encore which was apparent, when they were in power before. They have also not been blamed for any international terrorism yet, and do not want to be.

As of now, instead of flying planes into buildings in US cities, al-Qaeda is trying to rest on a model of competitive governance, and protection of communities, that feel marginalised, vulnerable, or threatened by forces who they dislike. This will also result as another feather in the cap for the Taliban, to maintain a 'smooth de-facto relationship,' which historically runs deep anyway.

After tasting power, the Taliban introduced the same theocratic rules that they applied in rural areas when the civilian government was functioning. It includes girls-only education in primary school, sanitised curriculums, women employed only in essential services, such as education and health, no mixing of genders, a ban on leaving home alone for women, enforcement of burqa, no TV, no music, compulsory attendance at mosques, and so on.

January 28, 2022

6

RUSSIA'S OFFENSIVE IN UKRAINE

When around a hundred thousand Russian troops were amassed near the Ukrainian border by December 2021, it created a renewal of a protracted civil war that first happened in 2014, in Russia's annexation of Crimea. Satellite imagery, as per Ukrainian intelligence, showed movements of armour, missile, and other heavy weaponry to Donbas separatist forces by Russia. In response, Ukrainian forces, in snow-laden wastelands were seen donning their white uniforms, with many snipers on the prowl. Near the front lines, war-weary soldiers were seen preparing food in makeshift kitchens, and the scenario reflected a newer version of Tolstoy's War and Peace.

The escalation in 2021 first happened in April when NATO first backed a Ukrainian offensive in its civil war against Russian-allied separatists in the eastern provinces, of Donetsk and Luhansk. That is when Russia moved more troops to its borders with Ukraine, signalling it would defend its allies in Donbas.

Former CIA Case Officer and CAM columnist John Kiriakou reported that the actual number of troops amassed on the Ukrainian border, estimated between seventy to ninety thousand, in April 2021, which was the same for the last eight years. For commentators, the long crises, anyhow, are the most intense since the cold war. The war, if happens, would be reminiscent of Bosnia and

Chechnya.

In December 2021, Russia created two draft treaties that contained requests of what it referred to as 'security guarantees' including a legally binding promise that Ukraine would not join the North Atlantic Treaty Organisation (NATO) as well as a reduction in NATO troops and military hardware stationed in Eastern Europe.

It also threatened an unspecified military response if those demands were not met in full. The United States and other NATO members have rejected these requests and warned Russia of swift and severe economic sanctions should it further invade Ukraine. Bilateral US-Russia diplomatic talks were held in January 2022, but those failed to defuse the crisis.

Troops on both sides have been facing each other down across this line of contact since a ceasefire ended large-scale combat in 2015. Fourteen thousand people have died because of Russia's war on Ukraine, which emerged in the aftermath of Ukraine's Euromaidan Revolution in 2013.

Also, two million people from the self-declared separatist region in Donbas have been displaced, fleeing to Ukraine and Russia. Yet, thousands of Ukrainian citizens continue to cross the line of contact between the uncontrolled Donbas territories and Ukraine every day. There are press stories which narrate how people of the self-declared people's republics of Donetsk and Lugansk in eastern Ukraine suffer under a complete economic blockade by Ukraine and its Western allies. A series of mysterious arrests, deaths and disappearances of self-declared public officials and field commanders in the territories has been followed by the appointment of figures with closer ties to Moscow. Though Moscow has increased control, the territories remain a grey zone for civil and workers' rights, as well as for opaque and criminal businesses. More than 700,000 Russian passports have now been issued to residents of the territories, which Ukraine's President Volodymyr Zelenskyy has called a 'sign of annexation'.

With some NATO member states hinting that they will not send troops to support Ukraine in the face of a Russian invasion, one of the last arrows in the quiver of those looking to deter the aggression from the Kremlin is the threat of economic isolation. Sanctions that have been proposed include removing Russia from the SWIFT banking sector and banning imports of Russian oil and gas. After the annexation of Crimea, the Russian economy was hit with a range of targeted, but limited sanctions on key industries.

George Voloshin, an expert on the economy of Russia and other post-Soviet states, warns that there are no sanctions left to put on Russia that would not also have serious blowback on Western countries. 'Going further with sanctions would be painful for everyone involved. We're at a stage where you've used all the small arms in your economic arsenal – now you need to use a bazooka,' he said, to Open Democracy.

Add to that, another option would be for European stakeholders to cancel the Nord Stream 2 pipeline project, which would carry gas under the Baltic Sea directly from Russia to Germany, bypassing Ukraine. This pipeline dramatically lowers Kyiv's leverage in any dispute.

For dodging sanctions, Russia has been making some rainy-day preparations for its economy to withstand more sanctions, including developing a domestic equivalent to

SWIFT banking.

The Russian government also appears to be preparing to argue that a military conflict, was started by Ukraine and its Western allies. For instance, Russian defence minister Sergey Shoigu claimed that US mercenaries were planning a chemical warfare attack in Donbas in late December 2021.

Despite all this, there are diplomatic channels existing intended to make peace. The first is the Trilateral Contact Group, which includes representatives of Ukraine, Russia and the Organisation for Cooperation and Security in Europe (OSCE). The group first met in June 2014, and signed an agreement in Minsk, Belarus, later that year.

The Trilateral Contact Group met again in Minsk and signed a new agreement known as Minsk 2. This agreement set out a plan for a ceasefire and later reintegration of the occupied Donetsk and Luhansk territories via elections, a special status in Ukraine's constitution and an amnesty for those who had participated in the armed uprising.

The second principal channel is the Normandy Format, comprising Ukraine, Russia, France, and Germany. This is a series of talks linked to the Minsk agreements. There are also the NATO Russia Council and OSCE talks with Russia.

Although, the problem with the Minsk2 agreement is that Ukrainian officials have called the document not binding under international law. Russia considers it binding. The Ukrainian authorities are reluctant to recognise any special status for the territories outside of its control, as it would give Russia leverage over Ukrainian territory. Previously, public protests have broken out in Ukraine over concerns of capitulation to Russia. That is why these peace protocols are not having the desired effect.

At this point, it seems plausible that a military operation from Russia against Ukraine would not require too many casualties among Russian soldiers, but it will most probably be televised, the 'sofa war', as it is called in Russia, and it is likely to receive approval among Russians.

What works in Russia's favour is that after the outbreak of hostilities in 2014, Ukraine's military had been hollowed out due to decades of corruption and underinvestment.

Ukraine's senior military staff still privately grumble that they were given advice by their Western military advisers not to contest Putin's annexation of Crimea, a decision that many remain bitter over.

When Ukrainian forces attempted to retake major separatist-held territories in early 2015, they were encircled and suffered a rout at the Battle of Debaltseve. It was this defeat that forced Ukraine to start negotiations, and temporarily abandon ambitions to regain control of its territory through military means.

Ukrainian military observers, however, are increasingly convinced that Russia will limit itself to a targeted escalation in the existing eastern battlegrounds rather than risk full-scale war. A widely circulated report by the Centre for Defence Strategies, a leading Ukrainian think tank, said that an offensive designed at capturing Ukraine is unlikely based on current troop movements. They estimated that around 66 battalions' worth of strength is amassed on the borders, but that Russia would need perhaps double this to overwhelm Ukraine. It would take around three weeks to prepare a force of that size. Russian troops have also not been organised into the battalion groups that would be used in a war, yet.

When it comes to the US, it says that there is no need to renegotiate Minsk 2. What is controversial on their part is that there are press reports which propagate that CIA since 2015 had secretly trained elite Ukrainian Special Forces units in firearms, camouflage techniques, land navigation, tactics like cover and move, intelligence and other areas.

As per an article by Marwan Bishara in Al Jazeera, NATO seems to be back united under Biden's leadership, and the scenario creates some important developments. Bishara went on to write: 'Biden, the Cold War liberal, is finally being taken seriously in Europe and Russia, as he uses the Putin scare to get the reluctant Europeans back in line behind the US. Even the leading European powers, France and Germany, that openly seek autonomy and even independence from the US in security affairs, are now following in Washington's footsteps, albeit unenthusiastically.' But, the US, like other NATO member states also says that it will not militarily help Ukraine if it is attacked, as it is not a NATO member.

So, US's priorities are self-limited, despite the claims that it is believed that the CIA is heavily involved in Ukraine, in addition to US's official aid to Ukraine since 2014, which amounts to nearly $2.4 billion.

China has already called for calm, making it clear that it opposes NATO's expansion to the Russian border. But Beijing also has a personal stake in Moscow's success against Washington in Ukraine, as it would pave the way for its own success against the US in Taiwan, and the rest of Asia.

The UK, on the hand, wants to fully support its allies in Ukraine, if Russia invades Ukraine, as the British army leads the NATO battle group in Estonia.

Alongside Russia and the US, the UK was also a signatory to the 1994 Budapest Memorandum, in which Ukraine relinquished its nuclear arsenal in exchange for security and political guarantees. Germany, contrarily, has a difficult relationship with Russia currently, as it is governed by Social Democrats since the 2021 election. They think the current Russian regime is not reliable, and that its last chancellor, Gerhard Schroder, betrayed European and German strategic interests by siding so closely with Putin and Gazprom, the Russian state-owned gas company. France, under Macron, in contrast, is keen to claim the mantle of leadership and speak in the name of Europe, by talking with Putin through direct telephone calls. But there are also further, internal divides among European countries, such as between the current Hungarian government, probably the staunchest supporter of Russia in Europe, and the Baltic states, which are at the most critical end. Further differences of interests exist between southern (especially Italy) and northern (Finland and Sweden) EU states. Nonetheless, the EU has passed unanimous sanctions against Russia in the past, and now the overall message is that much more incisive sanctions are on the table if Russia attacks Ukraine.

January 30, 2022

7

ARAB WORLD'S FIRST FEMALE PRIME MINISTER IN TUNISIA

By installing Raoudha Boudent Ramadhane, a politically unknown, as Tunisia's first woman prime minister, President Kais Saied showed his intentions of not taking a long-time grab at power. Earlier, there were howls about an extended coup. This announcement was a breathing room for the entire international community.

As months passed by since July 2021, Tunisians got concerned about where their democracy was heading, due to a lack of clear-cut political plans. They earlier had been disillusioned about the bickering of the ruling political coalition. However, Saied had failed in delivering what his nation required: economic prosperity. But now, it seemed there was another attempt at breaking the deadlock, as Tunisia has been mostly in political limbo since ousting of Ben Ali in 2011.

Many observers argued that as the country has been the birthplace of Arab spring, the first Arab female prime minister had to be in Tunisia. But, Ramadhane, a 63-year-old professor at the Tunis National School of Engineering, can claim this only in recent history. For hundreds of years, and until the beginning of the 20th century, it was not rare for women to rule in the Arab world, the most famous of which are Balqees, the Queen of Sheba, who ruled present-day Yemen five thousand years ago, and Fatima al

Zamil, from the powerful Shammar tribe. History books are also full of names of other prominent, strong-willed women who ruled powerful Arab states.

Hela Yousfi, a sociology lecturer at Paris Dauphine University, reflected that the appointment was not surprising, as Saied himself is a law professor turned politician. She went on to comment in an interview with Guardian: 'Kais Saied was brought to power by a popular extra-parliamentary movement, which expressed its total mistrust of the political class. So, there is a consistency there with the nomination of someone from outside the political class. It is consistent with the Tunisian people's complete crisis of faith in the political class, which has failed for 10 years to fulfil the aspirations of the Tunisian revolution.'

Tunisia has set an example because women have always taken a backseat in politics in the Arab world, after First World War. Due to feminist policies since 1956, the role of women is encouraged in the country. The policies were institutionalised by Habib Bourguiba, who enacted a revolutionary Personal Status Code, (PSC), brushing off opposition from religious and conservative leaders. This law gave women unprecedented rights, unheard of even in Western countries, such as the right to abortion, to prevent polygamy, and the right to divorce. As Bourguiba was a staunch secular himself, he perhaps is often said to be influenced by his second wife, Wassila Ben Ammar, a highly educated daughter of a bourgeois family. During Bourguiba's ill health, Wassila was the woman in charge, and she took all important policy decisions, including the appointment of Prime Minister Mohammad Mzali in 1980.

At the present, Tunisian women have roles in nearly every

profession, and one has even run for president. The 2014 constitution guarantees women and men 'equal rights and duties' without discrimination, and by extension, the country has one of the most progressive electoral gender quota laws in the world. Already in the 1950s, women were allowed to vote and run for office.

There have been other recent legislative victories since the revolution, notably a 2017 law aimed at cracking down on violence against women. But, for Sarah Medini, a political analyst, there was still a huge amount of work to be done 'on a practical level' to ensure significant changes were implemented. Although, many argue, after looking at her CV, that she was sworn in as prime minister for her competence, and not because of her gender. She oversaw education reforms in the previous two governments and has had a reasonable experience with the World Bank.

For Valentine Moghadam, a professor at Northeastern University, she will remain an inspiration to women in the Middle East and North Africa, and her appointment is more than a fig leaf. According to her, she can bring analytical and problem-solving skills to the role, as well as a network of contacts.

There was other leading Arab academia too that called for her support. For example, Professor Farouk El-Baz, retired director of the Centre for Remote Sensing at Boston University and a member of the presidential advisory council that advises Egyptian President Abdel Fattah el-Sisi, believed that her appointment was a 'welcome first', assuring 'Arab populations everywhere that the Tunisian leadership respects education and knowledge.'

Some others on the Tunisian streets, such as retirees, had an opposite viewpoint. They rather wanted a strong man of confidence and integrity, who knows the needs of the people and had the ability to lead the government.

On the political level, President Saied described Bouden-Ramadhane's appointment as 'historic and an honour for Tunisia and a tribute to Tunisian women.' But his critics argue that he made her appointment just to appease those who want him to address the gender gap, 'by dropping his opposition to a highly contentious law so that inheritance rights are equalised.'

If one talks of Tunisian wages, at the present, they are underwhelming. Tunisian academics earn less than minimum wage salary, which barely satisfies their middle-class lifestyle. Several Tunisian activists, therefore, are calling for a dialogue aimed at radical and real reforms in the sector as well.

When Saied first announced a political purge by suspending the parliament, he even arrested several political opponents, imposed travel bans, and invoked limitations, on businesspeople and judges.

Despite propagating his coup as temporary, he rejected calls for dialogue and faced mounting criticism from political parties, civil society, and media personalities, including some who had supported him.

Also, Saied in September 2021, announced that he himself would take the task of appointing the cabinet, stating that the constitutional provisions will not apply to him, showing his autocratic tendencies.

Going by the voice of many Tunisian people, they think Ramadhane has some serious work cut out for her. They wonder how a political novice will be able to create social and economic reforms which Tunisia desperately needs.

February 1, 2022

8

YEMEN WAR CONTINUES THROUGH DIFFERENT ACTORS

The grotesque war in Yemen entered a critical juncture in January 2022 when the Saudi-led coalition launched a series of air strikes at a prison facility. It was retaliation by Saudis for a missile and a drone attack, against the United Arab Emirates, in an industrial district of Abu Dhabi. Houthis called the reason for the attack on the prison facility 'baseless' and 'unfounded'. But Saudis believed that they had attacked a facility which was not placed on the No Strike List, and that it did not adhere to international humanitarian laws. Although, the killing of civilians tells a different story.

According to Medecins Sans Frontieres statements in Financial Times, Al Gumhouriyeh Hospital was so overwhelmed that it could not take patients. This is the second time, after a period of some months when Houthis also suffered headcount losses. In October 2021, when Houthis tried to seize Marib, an oil-rich northern Yemen region, it suffered heavy casualties then, too. At that time, even many of their military vehicles were destroyed.

Andrew England, who wrote a column for Financial Times, heard from his colleague Ahmed Mahat, head of MSF in Yemen that many civilian bodies at the scene of the strike during January 2022 were still missing. He also ascertained that it was impossible to believe how many civilians had been killed. Some sources say that the toll is by far the highest in three years.

When another air strike, in the same month, destroyed a telecommunications facility, in Hodeidah, a port region controlled by Houthis, the Internet was down all over Yemen, as TeleYemen, a state-monopolised company got affected.

A cut to the undersea FALCON cable project in 2020 also got similar outages. Since the advent of civil war, land cables to Saudi Arabia have been affected as well, while connections to two other undersea cables have not been finalised yet, due to the ongoing conflict.

In an interview with The New Arab, UN special envoy Hans Grundberg warned the UN security council that recent attacks by the Houthis on the UAE and Saudi Arabia 'indicate how this conflict risks spiralling out of control unless serious efforts are urgently made by the Yemeni parties, the region and the international community to end the conflict.' He also pointed out that aid agencies were quickly running out of money, forcing them to slash life-saving programs.

As UN World Food Program reduced food rations for 8 million people in December 2021, those 8 million people may get no food at all, or just a reduced ration in future. Starting in March 2022, the UN may also have to cancel most humanitarian flights in Yemen. Funding shortages could also deprive 3.6 million people of safe drinking water, end programs to combat gender-based violence and promote reproductive health.

The UN describes Yemen as the world's worst man-made crisis, as two hundred thousand have been directly or indirectly killed. Yet, some naive analysts challenge this notion as a 'potentially misleading oversimplification.' They fail to realise about the mounting tally of the dead, about the spreading cholera epidemic spiking up to 2.5 million cases, and the infrastructure that has turned into rubble. In fact, civilian deaths and injuries in Yemen's war have almost doubled since the UN human rights monitors were controversially removed in October 2021. And, in 2020 alone, around fifteen hundred Houthi child soldiers died. In fact, when it comes to dead children in Yemen, their tally comes up to ten thousand.

The situation has also worsened under the years-long de facto land, sea, and air blockade imposed by coalition forces, which has obstructed the flow of vital supplies of food and medicine. The blockade also contributes to an ongoing fuel crisis that has helped drive up the prices of essential goods.

The roots of the Yemen conflict lie in the fuel price hikes that first happened in 2014, when the Hadi government lifted fuel subsidies. It made Houthis launch a protest movement, which was countered by another movement that was loyal to Hadi and al-Islah party in the south. When Houthis took control of much of Sanaa in 2014, the Hadi government eventually resigned in January 2015, and Hadi later fled to Saudi Arabia. Then, a military division happened, with Saleh's forces aligning themselves with Houthis while remaining others remained loyal to the Hadi government. In 2015, Saudi Arabia joined through military campaigns to restore the Hadi administration. But what made the Yemen war more complex is the killing of Saleh by Houthis in December 2017, on suspicions of treason.

For its advantage, Saudi Arabia cobbled together a coalition of Sunni-majority Arab states: Bahrain, Egypt,

Jordan, Kuwait, Morocco, Qatar, Sudan, and the United Arab Emirates. By 2018, the coalition had expanded to include forces from Eritrea and Pakistan, mainly to reinstate the Hadi government. But observers also say that due to friction between these actors, the war is prolonged. The war also made Iran retaliate.

In this war, other extremist groups working in an alienated manner such as Al-Qaeda in the Arab Peninsula, have even benefitted from the recent chaos. In 2015, the group captured Mukalla, a coastal city, and released three hundred of the group's inmates from prison. The militant group then expanded its control westward to Aden, and seized parts of the city, before coalition forces recovered much of the region in 2016. AQAP has also provided Yemenis in some areas with security and public services unfulfilled by the state, which has strengthened support for the group.

For years, AQAP vied for influence with the Houthis and the self-declared Islamic State, especially in the central al-Bayda Governorate.

The Islamic State marked its 2015 entrance into Yemen with suicide attacks on two Zaydi mosques in Sanaa, which killed close to one hundred forty worshippers. Though the group has claimed other high-profile attacks, including the assassination of Aden's governor in late 2015, its following lags that of AQAP.

Also, the al-Islah party has had a newly founded relationship with Saudi Arabia, after its support for Operation Desert Storm. For this, they incurred heavy losses from the Houthis, who launched a campaign of kidnappings against al-Islah leaders. According to an article by Mutahar Al Sofari, in Washington Institute:

'Saudi Arabia's relationship with Islah Party, an Islamist party, condemned for its affiliation with Muslim Brotherhood, is exceptional because it contrasts against Saudi Arabia led coalition's approach to the Muslim Brotherhood generally. As of now, the relationship defies conventional diplomatic boundaries in the region, and yet, it has continued to survive, and both parties have shown a willingness to sacrifice for the sake of the relationship.' However, cracks also appeared when the al-Islah party tried to present the war in Yemen as 'political' rather than 'sectarian', as the Saudi press has done.

The US, throughout its course in the war, conducted about one hundred eighty-five strikes over eight years under Barack Obama, while the Trump administration launched nearly two hundred strikes in its four years. But, the US. strikes have also resulted in the deaths of more than one hundred civilians, watchdog groups say. According to an article by Kali Robinson in Council on Foreign Relations: 'the United States has backed the Saudi-led coalition, as have France, Germany, and the United Kingdom. US interests include the security of Saudi borders; free passage in the Bab al-Mandeb strait, the choke point between the Arabian and Red Seas and a vital artery for the global transport of oil; and a government in Sanaa that will cooperate with US counterterrorism programs.'

When it comes to the drafting agreements, the 2018 Stockholm Agreement averted a battle in the vital port city of Hodeidah, but there has been little success in implementing the accord's provisions, which include the exchange of more than fifteen thousand prisoners and the creation of a joint committee to de-escalate violence in the city of Taiz.

Many experts even argue that viewing the war as a two-party proxy conflict, as exemplified by UN Security Council Resolution 2216, is unproductive given the fragmentation of anti-Houthi forces, and the involvement of foreign powers. Peace talks that involve more political parties and civil society groups could level the playing field.

February 17, 2022

9

A JOINT PATROL MISSION IN SYRIA

In January 2022, the Russian Defence Ministry announced that its air force had begun joint patrols with Syrian military pilots along Syria's borders. As reported by Al Arabiya News, the patrols involved fighter jets, fighter-bombers, and airborne early warning aircraft, flying routes from the Golan Heights through southern Syria and then along the Euphrates River up to the north. Moscow presented these patrols as demonstrations of solidarity with the Assad regime and as measures to help Damascus pre-emptively counter threats. They also served Russia's longer-term goal of assisting Assad in regaining control over territory still held by opposition groups.

Adam Lammon, writing for the Centre for the National Interest, argued that the patrols were designed to enhance the Syrian military's independent capabilities, asserting sovereignty while reducing Russia's operational burden. Paul Iddon in Forbes offered a more nuanced interpretation, suggesting that Russia may have timed the patrols to coincide with a break in winter weather, anticipating that Israel could exploit such conditions to launch strikes in Syria. He added that the patrols along the Golan Heights were likely intended as a warning to Israel, following its December 2021 airstrikes on Latakia port, which had already irritated Moscow.

Israel's air campaign against Iran-linked targets in Syria has been ongoing for nearly a decade. As Reuters reported, Israel has repeatedly struck Hezbollah positions and Iranian militias, including several attacks on Latakia in 2013, 2014 and 2018, the latter sparking heightened tensions with Russia due to its military presence in the area. These joint patrols, therefore, were interpreted in Tel Aviv as alarming developments. Israeli military officers reportedly engaged Damascus in talks to defuse tensions, but the underlying reality remained: Israel was determined to prevent Iranian entrenchment in Syria, while Russia sought to balance its ties with both Assad and Israel.

The political backdrop was equally fraught. In October 2021, Israeli Prime Minister Naftali Bennett declared that Israel would retain the Golan Heights, captured in 1967, regardless of international opinion.

As The Guardian noted, Bennett pledged to double the Israeli population in the Golan, equalling the Druze Arab community, and later emphasised to Vladimir Putin that relations between Israel and Russia were vital, citing the million Russian speakers in Israel. Putin congratulated Bennett on his premiership, underscoring the importance Moscow placed on maintaining dialogue with Tel Aviv. Since 2015, Israel and Russia had operated a de-confliction mechanism to avoid clashes in Syria, though incidents still occurred.

Iran and Syria, however, have long complained that Moscow does not fully share their views. Russia only occasionally condemns Israeli strikes as destabilising, and often refrains from stronger action.

Anton Mardasov wrote in Al-Monitor that this ambivalence reflects Russia's desire to avoid direct confrontation with Israel and, by extension, the United States. Moscow recognises that maintaining cordial ties with Israel reduces the risk of escalation with Washington, even if it frustrates Assad and Tehran.

The issue of air defence systems illustrates this tension. Russia supplied Syria with S-300 systems, but has been reluctant to allow their full operational use. Analysts noted that Moscow appears to retain control over these systems, preventing Damascus from firing them during Israeli raids. This reluctance suggests that Russia wants to avoid a direct clash between Israel and Syria, even as it stages joint patrols to project solidarity.

From Tehran's perspective, the patrols are welcome. Iranian officials see them as reducing Damascus's reliance on Iran, while still bolstering Assad's position. Russia's presence in Syria since 2015 has already turned the tide of the war in Assad's favour, and Moscow continues to view its bases at Khmeimim and Tartus as strategic assets, projecting power into the Mediterranean and complicating NATO's southern flank.

Yet Russia's ambitions extend beyond Syria. Anton Mardasov in Al-Monitor reported that in December 2021, Moscow moved more than twenty aircraft and helicopters from Khmeimim to airfields in Hasakah and Deir ez-Zor, with A-50 AWACS aircraft coordinating operations. This manoeuvre placed Russian forces closer to US positions, heightening tensions rather than easing them. Mardasov argued that Russia lacks the capacity to deploy thousands of troops quickly, given its modest fleet of transport aircraft and limited ocean-going warships. Nevertheless, these moves were intended to demonstrate that Russia's military grouping in Syria was more than symbolic: it was a platform for projecting influence into Venezuela, Africa and beyond.

Despite these efforts, foreign air forces continue to operate freely over Syrian skies. The United States, Turkey and Israel regularly conduct missions, often with precision strikes against Syrian aircraft. Decades of attrition have left Syria's air force depleted, its planes visibly worn and vulnerable. The joint patrols were meant to exhibit Syrian sovereignty, but in practice they underscored Damascus's dependence on Moscow.

The logic of Russia's joint patrols, therefore, is layered. On one level, they are about demonstrating solidarity with Assad and signalling deterrence to Israel. On another, they are about reducing Russia's operational burden by training Syrian pilots and asserting Syrian sovereignty. At the same time, they are about balancing Moscow's relations with Israel, Iran, and the United States. As Paul Iddon in Forbes observed, the patrols were as much about political messaging as military utility. They conveyed Russia's annoyance at Israeli strikes, reassured Assad of Moscow's support, and reminded Washington of Russia's enduring presence in Syria.

Yet the contradictions remain stark. Russia wants to appear as Assad's protector, but it hesitates to confront Israel directly. It wants to reduce its burden in Syria, but it cannot fully trust Assad's forces to operate independently. It wants to project power against NATO and the US, but its logistical limitations constrain its reach. And it wants to balance ties with Iran, but Tehran's ground presence often undermines Moscow's diplomatic manoeuvres.

Ultimately, the joint patrols of January 2022 were emblematic of Russia's broader strategy in Syria: a careful balancing act between deterrence and restraint, projection, and pragmatism. They were less about changing the military balance than about signalling Russia's determination to remain a central player in Syria's skies. For Assad, they offered reassurance; for Israel, they raised alarms; for Iran, they promised reduced reliance; and for Washington, they underscored the persistence of Russian influence.

February 19, 2022

10

BURKINA FASO IS ANOTHER COUP VICTIM IN AFRICA

Burkina Faso's army announced in late January 2022 that it had deposed President Roch Kabore, the government, and the national assembly. It also suspended the constitution. On a state television, the army officers blustered that the coup had been done without carrying out violence in the country, and those detained were kept in a secure location. The statements, signed by Colonel Paul Henri Sandaogo, were made in the name of a previously unheard entity, the Patriotic Movement for Safeguard and Restoration or MPSR, according to its French language acronym. The army even chaired a 15-person technical committee charged with proposing a timeline for a transitional government that would lead the country to elections soon.

The coup was planned because of Kabore's inability to keep the nation together, mainly after twenty-seven-year rule of Compaore. There was also a failed coup in 2015, but this time the army was successful in attaining power.

According to press reports by Al Jazeera, the army broadcast came after two days of confusion and fear in the capital Ouagadougou, where heavy gunfire erupted at army camps, with soldiers demanding more support to fight against various jihadist armed groups. Burkina Faso's coup also came amid an escalation in attacks linked to al-Qaeda, and ISIS groups, which have killed thousands, and displaced around 1.5 million people. The number of extremist attacks has risen from nearly 500 in 2020 to more than 1,150 in 2021, placing Burkina Faso well ahead of Mali's 684 and Niger's 149 violent events. There were also some civilian protests in January 2022 which were met with suppression.

Invoking international reactions, United Nations chief Antonio Guterres said in a statement that he 'strongly condemns any attempted takeover of government by the force of arms.' The United States reacted by saying that it was 'deeply concerned' about developments in Burkina Faso, and urged a swift return to civilian rule. When it comes to African Union and the West African bloc ECOWAS, they also pledged that they will hold the military responsible for Kabore's safety.

Adama Gaye, a Senegalese political commentator, told Al Jazeera that 'the failure to govern' was at the heart of these recent events. 'Anybody who has been monitoring the evolution of Burkina Faso expected this to happen, the writing was on the wall, clearly,' Gaye said, about the military moves.

It was Lieutenant Colonel Paul Henri Sandaogo Damiba who was inaugurated as president in February 2022, where he was dressed in a camouflage uniform, a red beret, and wore a sash in the colours of Burkina Faso's national flag.

The ex-ruler Kabore was elected in 2015 following a popular revolt. He was re-elected in 2020, but the following year faced a wave of anger over the mounting toll from an increasingly conflict that has spilt over from neighbouring Mali.

The move has been largely welcomed on the streets. It shows how exasperated the Burkinabe people have become with Kabore's leadership as the country has endured years of deteriorating security amid a region wide

Islamist insurgency. It was something like what Guineans felt during the last coup there.

What mainly led to Kabore demise is his debauch spending on military expenditures. Burkina Faso's military expenditures have more than doubled under Kabore, from roughly $150 million when he first took office in 2015, to $382 million in 2020, according to the Stockholm International Peace Research Institute. It has been the United States which also has been supporting Burkina Faso with military spending since 2009, as part of America's 9/11 counter-terrorism goals. This support also kind of led to groundwork for increased militarism. In response to the last coup, the United States halted $160 million in aid.

In contrast to the deposed president, Damiba has sought to present himself as an expert in countering terrorism. A graduate of the military academy in Paris, he is the author of a book titled West African Armies and Terrorism: Uncertain Responses in which he analysed anti-terrorism strategies in the Sahel region and their limits. However, his plan for battling the armed groups remains unclear. Military rule, in fact, will exacerbate the problems in Burkina Faso that have allowed extremism to thrive.

Colonial powers have also had a say in Burkina Faso's political circles. Paris had expanded its military cooperation at ex-President Kabore's request, including the country's involvement in its Operation Barkane battling armed groups in Africa Sahel's region.

After the coup, it also remains unclear whether Damiba may turn to Russia for security cooperation. Moscow, always, has been looking for an alternative to Western intervention. But, one of the facts, that remains highly unchallenged is blind support to ruling regimes by outside powers, whether dictatorial leaders, or the military, for gaining access to natural resources.

February 21, 2022

11

TURKEY'S PRESENCE INSIDE NORTHERN SYRIA

Turkey has retained a military presence in northern Syria, after it launched its first border operation in August 2016, through Operation Euphrates Shield to fight Islamic State near Turkey's border, and to also prevent Syrian Democratic Forces (SDF) from advancing further westward.

Turkey completed Euphrates Shield after capturing the city of Al-Bab from Islamic State in March 2017. Turkish allied militia and the Turkish army control these regions. Turkey has launched a total of four of its military operations since 2016. All its major ground operations needed to be carefully deconflicted with Moscow. The last one, in 2019, also required coordination with a chaotic Trump White House. While Trump first gave the green light, he later changed his tune and threatened Turkey with heavy sanctions. Such discord on the American front made Turkish-Russian coordination even more essential for Ankara.

Ankara has even invested in a lot of infrastructural projects in the Euphrates Shield Zone. Turkish Lira is, in fact, already a currency in northern Syria.

In 2017, under the framework of the Astana agreement with Russia and Iran, Turkey began establishing its troop presence in Syria's Idlib province via the establishment of twelve observation posts manned by the Turkish army. The aims of the deployment were the prevention of clashes between Assad regime forces, and armed opposition groups that control Idlib, the most powerful being the Hayat Tahrir al-Sham.

However, Turkey's subsequent incursions into northern Syria have been mostly controversial. In early 2018, it occupied Afrin, which was initially controlled by YPG. Then, in October 2019, Turkey invaded a large swathe of northeastern Syria, previously controlled by the SDF. It has resulted in the displacement of thousands of people, helping its Syrian proxies loot civilian homes and businesses. It was also the Turkish government that settled two hundred thousand Arab refugees from Ghouta, in homes and areas which were once possessed by Kurds.

Kyle Orton, an independent Middle East analyst noted the situation and raised an important point: 'Unwilling, for political and economic reasons, to use its own troops in significant numbers, Turkey works through former rebel groups that now have no cause beyond the Turkish pay cheque, which inter alia diminishes their incentives to behave well towards the populace.' This has set up a high degree of lawlessness by these rebels, who create a scenario where many civilians are killed in the crossfire.

Turkey's occupation of northern Syria is assessed very differently by different groups in the region. For Kurds, Turkey's incursions, and rule have been a disaster. The expulsion of Kurds in places like Afrin and Ras al Ayn, and the settlement of Arab refugees in homes where Kurds once lived is nothing but ethnic cleansing.

For Syrian Turkmen, however, the Turkish military

presence seems godsend.

When it comes to many Sunni Arab Syrians, they view Turkey's presence in the region as a lesser evil to the return of the Assad regime to these areas. This is the case with several north Aleppo and Idlib provinces.

Domestically, Ankara has used the Syrian conflict as a pretext to suppress the rights of the Kurds living in Turkey as well and has limited their parliamentary representation to secure a landmark constitutional reform in 2017.

Many rebel militias have now joined the Turkish constituted, Syrian National Army. It reflects the expression of their loyalty to Turkey so that they overthrow the government in Damascus and take control of Syria one day.

According to Nicolas Heras, director of government relations at the Institute for the Study of War, Turkey has 'set the foundation for a long-term presence in northern Syria similar to its presence in Cyprus.' Idlib seems to be the first territory that the world should likely expect to be incorporated as if it is a de facto part of Turkey. It will result in a threat to long-term stability in the region.

Heras further went to comment in an interview with The New Arab: 'all-in-all, the Turkish-controlled areas of northern Syria are a patchwork of regions ranging from tightly managed, de facto extensions of Turkish provinces, to chaos zones ruled by predatory Syrian rebel warbands, to an al-Qaeda safe haven.'

In recent months, Erdogan increased his threats about a new military invasion in northern Syria, in the cities of Tel Rifaat and Manbij.

In foreign policy terms, Turkey's military operations in Syria have resulted in increasingly tense relations with the United States. Washington's support for the Syrian Kurds has alienated Ankara to a deeper extent. At the same time, Ankara's involvement in Syria has also given Turkey new leverage over the EU when it comes to the management of refugee inflows.

Turkey's involvement in Syria has also equipped it with new tools for conducting a more aggressive and nationalistic foreign policy. It also means that ISIS does not present an existential threat to Turkey the way the PKK does. Ankara always welcomed jihadi infiltration of Syria by opening its borders wide, to make Syria fall to bits, reflecting a new Ottoman hegemony. After all, these jihadists were the most effective fighters against Turkey's main enemies in Syria: the Assad regime and secular Kurdish nationalists.

February 28, 2022

12

ISRAEL'S OBSERVER STATUS INSIDE AFRICAN UNION

Israel's observer status inside African Union granted in July 2021 has split many political institutions in the continent. An observer status for Israel gives them the privilege to participate in the organisation's activities, but they do not have the ability to vote or propose resolutions, showing that an observer status gives limited rights. However, through it, Israel will fine-tune its diplomatic relations in the continent.

The consequences of recognising Israel could be as important as the 1975 Resolution 77 (XII) by the Organisation of African Unity, the predecessor of the African Union, which recognised Zionism as a form of racism.

Historically, many experiences between Africans and Palestinians converged, as they saw liberation struggles in lieu of Western imperialism. This can be explained in the wording of the above-mentioned Resolution 77 (XII), which equated between 'the racist regime in occupied Palestine and the racist regimes in Zimbabwe and South Africa' as they are all grounded in the same 'common imperialist origin … (and are) organically linked in their policy aimed at the repression of the dignity and integrity of the human being.'

Realising this, Israel has worked diligently to strengthen its presence in Africa. Currently, forty-six of the fifty-five members of the African Union recognise Israel. Additionally, it operates seventeen embassies and twelve consulates throughout the continent. Some of Israel's latest diplomatic victories include ties with Chad in 2019 and Morocco and Sudan in 2020, all being Muslim-majority countries.

The diplomatic shift in Africa happened when they saw Palestine and other Arab countries 'doing business' with Israel. Many African countries felt that their solidarity was no longer serving a particular purpose. Africa's Israeli boycott, which initially began in 1973, faltered soon after the Palestinian leadership itself signed a series of agreements with Israel, starting with the Oslo Accords of 1993. Thus, there was an eventual revival of diplomatic ties with Tel Aviv.

Israel has been trying to win back observer status for twenty years, ever since it lost it when the Organisation of African Unity was disbanded in 2002, to make way for its replacement organisation, the African Union. Libyan leader Moammar Gaddafi was behind Israel's original ouster.

There is also little evidence to suggest that Palestinian Authority tried to win back many African countries by launching a coordinated counter-campaign. Nonetheless, the occupied Palestinian territory already has observer status at the African Union, and pro-Palestinian language is typically featured in statements delivered at the AU's annual summits.

According to Palestinian writer Ramzy Baroud, there is a renewed scramble for Africa, not only by Israel but also by Russia, China, and the United States, which has forced Africa to pursue pragmatic thinking, thereby abandoning the old discourse regarding colonial liberation and decolonisation. As Israel is projecting itself as a rising superpower, it has led Africa to buy unmanned drones, digital monitoring, and surveillance technology from them.

However, it was on February 2022, when PA Prime Minister Mohammed Shtayyeh retaliated at an African Union Summit, and called for withdrawal and objection to Israel's observer status. It was in July 2021, which had led Moussa Faki Mahamat, as Chairman of the African Union Commission, who decided to take it upon himself to grant Israel observer status. Those African states which did not toe his line were tainted as 'nations having double standards' by him. Despite this stance, the 2022 AU Summit also proved that there are some takers of Palestine in the continent, even though there are many shortcomings in the Palestinian leadership.

In truth, Faki had his own reasons to grant Israel the coveted status. The AU Commission Chairperson was Chad's Foreign Minister until 2017. Though Chad did not declare its diplomatic ties with Israel until 2019, he must have played a significant role in paving the way for the N'Djamena-Tel Aviv official connection.

Algeria and South Africa came to the rescue of Palestinians, but they failed to kick out Israel, as AU Commission argued that it acted within its 'full sphere of competence' reading of the AU document, setting out the criteria for granting observer status and the system of accreditation. This also gives a reason for the watchers to note that Israel is getting accepted in the global community, more easily than before.

AU has realised, in its own way that isolating Israel, will not promote the well-being of Palestinians, but this viewpoint will become a cause of disagreement for rejectionists anyhow.

The only thing that would work for Palestinians, in terms of working for rejection of Israel's African Union observer status, is to formulate counter strategies. Those strategies, include mobilising civil society organisations, by sending strong, collective messages that Israel is not welcomed in Africa. It is because a region mired by colonialism, neo-colonialism, and apartheid will pay a heavy moral price for itself if it does business with another colonial apartheid regime.

March 1, 2022

13

PUTIN CHOOSES WAR

For months, Putin denied that he would invade his Ukrainian neighbour. Even Ukrainian intelligence and its think tanks had made calculations that a large-scale war was not imminent, at the land border. But Putin shocked everyone, and eventually went ahead and chose war by land, air, and sea after a pre-dawn media address, as he thought Russians 'could not be safe, could not develop, and could not exist' for a while. He even claimed that his goal was to protect his people subjected to bullying, and genocide, and aimed for the demilitarisation and de-Nazification of modern Ukraine. For this, he even vowed to bring 'Ukrainian fascists' to court, who run the country since 2014. Although, Ukrainian leaders, including its prime minister, rejected Russia's slur, outrightly. But there are some Ukrainian territorial defence groups who are overtly and unabashedly hard-right in their ideological orientation. Militarily, forces like the infamous Azov Regiment have been active in southeastern Ukraine, though not exclusively. In the past, the Organisation of Ukrainian Nationalists (OUN-B) led by Stepan Bandera was also regarded by people in eastern Ukraine through Soviet historiography as neo-Nazi but facts of history largely negate this.

It was in 2020 when Putin wrote a long piece describing Russians and Ukrainians as one nation. He also described the collapse of the Soviet Union in 1991 as the disintegration of historical Russia. It was something which was reflective of the Tsarist rule in the 19th century.

Just as the US and its European allies used the UN-mandated 'Responsibility to Protect' (R2P) principle to justify their 'humanitarian' interventions in Libya, for example, Russia is referring to it to justify its intervention in Ukraine.

Putin has also all along felt bitter about Ukraine's move towards the European Union, as he thinks that NATO members are no innocent bystanders because they have not only deployed strike weapons near Russia's borders but also installed its forces and military infrastructure near eastern Europe, central Europe, and Baltic states. NATO, although, thinks if they would not have done this, Russia would attack Europe in future, starting with small territorial grabs, covert intrusions, including rapid attacks on a vulnerable corridor like Suwalki gap. However, Putin's assertions are unflagging for a while.

After the invasion, some analysts, seeing the naked territorial aggression, started making comparisons of Putin with Saddam Hussein, as both men resorted to expansionist ambitions. While Saddam Hussein's actions spoke of hostility towards Iran in the wake of its 1979 revolution, and Kuwait in 1990, Putin's actions spoke of invasions in Georgia in 2008, and Crimea in 2014.

The war on Ukraine had started when tanks rolled from Russia, Russia annexed Crimea, and its ally Belarus. Then, war became frightening, when missiles hit not only military infrastructure, but also civilian homes, and when warplanes started bombing major modern Ukrainian cities. It made thousands of common Ukrainians seek refuge in cold war era bomb shelters, as enormous plumes of black smoke billowed into the peachy daybreak skies. Over two thousand Ukrainian civilians have died since

Russia's invasion in February 2022. After five days after the invasion, nearly 660,000 people, mostly women and children fled Ukraine. It resulted in the most intense wave of migration since the 1990s. Up to four million people could flee, if the situation deteriorates further, according to UN estimates. Adding more woes, there were press reports by Time, where refugees of colour were dismayed by the continued preferential treatment for Ukrainians in the official Polish response and from ordinary Poles. As of now, there is also a lack of efficient humanitarian corridors.

Ever since the war began, a string of leading Western companies has exited Russia, Nord Stream 2 has gone insolvent, the oil prices have soared, and the world's largest shipping lines have halted Russian deliveries.

On the eve of the invasion, Zelensky had tried to telephone Putin to appeal for negotiations, but the Russian leader would not take the call. In the coming days, Zelensky would accuse Russia of 'nuclear terror', after a reckless attack on Zaporizhzhia nuclear power plant, the largest such facility in Europe.

After launching attacks on Ukraine's north, east and south, it seems Putin's long-term goals are unknown, although he denies installing a puppet regime from Kremlin. According to BBC, there is one unconfirmed report where it is believed that Putin aims to split Ukraine into two regions. A Macron aide, however, believes that he wants the 'whole of Ukraine'.

Since late 2021, Russia scrapped the 2015 peace deal for the east and recognised areas under rebel control as independent. In recognising the breakaway regions, the Kremlin claimed that it was supporting their right to self-determination, just as the West did for Croats,

Slovenes, Macedonians, and Bosnians during the breakup of Yugoslavia in the 1990s. His recognition of the two breakaway republics in eastern Ukraine is also reminiscent of US President Donald Trump's illegal recognition of Israeli sovereignty over the occupied Syrian Golan Heights, and occupied Palestinian East Jerusalem, which Biden continues to uphold.

There are also reports, according to Daily Mail, where it is believed that Russian mercenaries, the Wagner Group, will be flown from Africa to kill twenty-three key Ukrainian figures, including the Klitschko brothers, although Moscow denies this.

The scale and scope of the Ukrainian invasion seem more like Moscow's menacing power projections during the Cold War when the Soviet Union intervened in Hungary in 1956, Czechoslovakia in 1968 and Afghanistan in 1979.

In the first four days since Putin invaded Ukraine, the United States and European nations promised hundreds of millions of dollars in new arms. Germany, for the first time, vowed to supply five hundred Stinger anti-aircraft missiles and a thousand anti-tank weapons. But, with the capital under bombardment from four sides, delivering them to Kyiv will be a challenge. And, the new arms are unlikely to change the balance of military power significantly or quickly. The Ukrainian army remains outmanned and outgunned by Russia. Despite the inspiring Ukrainian resistance that has slowed the initial incursion, Moscow retains an edge. Russia's tactics have toughened as hospitals and other civilian infrastructure has repeatedly been hit by air raids and artillery shells.

Although, it is not just weapons that have been flown into Ukraine. About sixty thousand diasporas have returned to the country. Foreign fighters have also made their way inside Ukraine, who are driven by a variety of ideologies, and reasons. Russia has announced that it, too, will receive foreign fighters, mainly Syrians with experience in urban combat, to shore up its armed forces.

After the war, Russia also sacrificed economic goals for military aggression. It shows Russia is unfazed, seems prepared, and is not dissuaded by sanctions, no matter how severe, when it comes to pursuing its core national interests.

Critics such as Greg Yudin, a Moscow professor, argue that Putin felt his power ebbing, and chose war to save himself, not his country. He may be wrong on this because according to polls done by Levada Centre, Putin's popularity has spiked from 61% to 69%, hinting that most Russians support the war in Ukraine, and that anti-war protestors on the streets do not tell the real story.

March 3, 2022

14

FRANCE WITHDRAWS TROOPS FROM MALI

Due to multiple obstructions by the ruling Malian regime, France has decided to withdraw its troops from the country in February 2022. In fact, the decision applies not only to France's Barkhane force in the Sahel but also to the Takuba European force that Paris had been trying to forge along with its allies.

Macron promised that the withdrawal would be done in an orderly manner. It was in 2021 when Macron first promised a walkout from Mali if the country veered into radicalism. A European special mission is withdrawing, too. The withdrawal is expected to be in a four to six-month period.

The immediate cause is a diplomatic breakdown between France (and its allies) and the junta that overthrew Mali's elected government in 2020. The junta led a second coup in 2021 and has since refused to hand power to civilians. It wants to keep power till 2025. The junta also recently kicked out the French ambassador and Danish commandos, who were helping it fight the jihadists. Rubbing more salt to the wounds, the regime even hired Russian mercenaries from the Wagner Group, a move that gives Russia a foothold in the region.

But, according to an article by Jacqueville and Paris, in The Economist, the roots lie even deeper. France's campaign, which started so well, has been going badly. The Mali deployment has also been fraught with problems for

France. Of the fifty-three soldiers killed serving in its Barkhane mission in west Africa, forty-eight of them died in Mali. The jihadists have continued to grow, despite the French army and the regional armies having won tactical victories. Although, Macron has denied that the mission has been a failure, and instead blames Mali's coup leaders, and Chad for failing to fight extremism in the region.

Over the course of time, France was helped by European partners, such as the United Kingdom, Denmark, and Sweden, for providing crucial helicopter capabilities for air mobility. Other Europeans, including the Germans and the British, have sent troops to the U.N. peacekeeping mission in Mali, and smaller partners, such as Estonia and the Czech Republic, have shown highly important symbolic European solidarity by committing special forces to Takuba. France's withdrawal from Mali now creates a problem for the previous multinational efforts to stabilise it, as French help will be less readily available when they come under attack. Some other troop contributors may also be looking to back out.

Incidentally, the withdrawal of Western forces, a long-standing demand by Mali's al-Qaeda militants, could create some room for negotiations out of the insurgency. The withdrawal, also, will have security implications for other countries in the Sahel region, who have been grappling with their own jihadist insurgencies.

French first arrived in Mali in 2013. It was a mad rush from bases in Senegal, Chad, and Burkina Faso at that time. As jihadists were poised to capture Bamako, the capital, within days, there was no time for a multinational force arriving from the UN or ECOWAS, the regional bloc. Frances Hollande, then French president, wanted them to 'get the job done'. Within hours they were attacking the jihadists, and within weeks France was recapturing cities such as Timbuktu and Gao. But, no one thought that this brief intervention would turn into a grinding nine-year-old struggle against Al-Qaeda and Islamic State. Before the troop pullout, Macron had been pushing for increased European military involvement alongside his forces.

It also shows how soaring the jihadist history in Mali is. After the ousting and killing of Libya's leader Muammar Gaddafi, Tuareg mercenaries who had been fighting for him returned home to Mali determined to fight for the independence of the north of the country. With Gaddafi's weapons, they formed an alliance with al-Qaeda-linked Islamists who were to become stronger partners. Together they took control of the north and threatened to seize control of the whole of Mali. In doing this, they exploited the political turmoil, poverty, and weakness of local authorities.

While the French intervention was meant to help Mali combat extremism, the crisis in the region has metamorphosed into an internal ethnic conflict. In the Mopti region, there is a conflict between the Fulani and Dogons, as well as between the Bambara and Fulani. In Timbuktu and Gao, there is a conflict between the Touaregs and Arabs on the one hand, and between the Touaregs and the Songhais on the other.

France will continue to fight jihadists in the region, but its task will be more difficult as the militants carve out more havens in and around Mali. It still is viewed as an 'occupying force,' and a colonial power.

The provocative question which arises now is whether Mali's neighbours can fight on their own, especially countries in the Gulf of Guinea. President Emmanuel Macron said that European forces would be centred on Niger, which will bring more balance to the fighting.

But, somehow, Western allies are realising a worrying defeat in the region. Observers also see the withdrawal as humiliating.

March 5, 2022

15

EXTRADITION APPEAL OF JULIAN ASSANGE

Journalism is not a crime. But, when Julian Assange's extradition to the United States became legal, it was a classic case of the attack on press freedom. Ironically, a court in London paved the way for Assange's prosecution on Human Rights Day. And, it is also cynical that all this happened on the day two journalists were awarded a Nobel Peace Prize in Oslo in December 2021. His fiancé, Stella Moris believed that his case is a 'grave miscarriage of justice.'

The prison, where he lived is called 'British Guantanamo' for its tough conditions. He was convicted there for breaching the conditions of his bail after his asylum was revoked by the Ecuadorian embassy in London. Some of the charges of his alleged disruptive behaviour inside the embassy were outrageous, according to his supporters, including smearing faeces on its walls.

The US had won its appeal against a January 2022 court ruling where it was said that he could be extradited due to concerns over his mental health. They charged him with violating the Espionage Act.

What Julian Assange did was basically that he divulged classified documents that proved the United States committing war crimes by exposing the abuses done by the US military. No one has been held accountable for those war crimes until now. Instead, a revenge ritual has been unleashed against a journalist to whom the world owes for those revelations.

While he was in prison, pledges were made that Assange will not be held under inhumane prison conditions. But his assassination plans concocted by the former US administration under Donald Trump made a mockery of those pledges. In fact, Yahoo! News made a report public in September 2021 that the CIA had plotted to poison, abduct or assassinate Assange in 2017. As a reaction, Kristinn Hrafnsson, current editor-in-chief of WikiLeaks, compared the alleged CIA plot to the Saudi assassination of a journalist, Jamal Khashoggi.

Assange's defence team will appeal the verdict but the case will drag on. However, Assange should not endure further proceedings sitting in a prison cell. He should rather be released immediately and placed under house arrest.

In other cases, the British legal system has done exactly that. The most prominent example is the case of the former Chilean dictator, Augusto Pinochet, a man responsible for the executions of thousands of regime opponents. When Spain demanded his extradition at the end of the 1990s, he was allowed to spend the 16 months of the proceedings in the comforts of a villa south of London, until he was released.

Assange is wanted on eighteen charges in the United States and faces a maximum 175-year prison sentence if convicted. His lawyers have long argued that the protracted case against him is politically motivated. And, Assange's supporters believed that he never sold out and remained true to his cause. He himself also denies any wrongdoing. His lawyers say he was acting as a journalist and is entitled to First Amendment freedom of the press protections for publishing documents that exposed the US military's wrongdoing in Iraq and Afghanistan.

According to BBC, Assange's team are likely to try to reverse this judgement in two ways. First, they want to challenge findings that his leaks amounted to an alleged crime, but it is not clear if such an appeal would be heard. Second, they may ask the British supreme court to examine judgement on the US's diplomatic assurances, but there is no guarantee it will take the case because they would have to argue that there is a fundamental problem with the law, which has never been the case in the past. So, time may be running out.

Nick Vamos, a partner at Peters & Peters solicitors in London and a former head of extradition at Britain's Crown Prosecution Service, gives a clearer picture. He told Al Jazeera that it was unlikely that the appeal would be granted because Assange's lawyers can only take the case to the supreme court if the high court rules that there are matters of 'general public importance' to consider.

The US had offered assurances, including that Julian Assange would not be subject to solitary confinement, pre- or post-trial or detained at the ADX Florence Supermax jail, a maximum-security prison in Colorado if extradited. Lawyers for the US said he would be allowed to transfer to Australia to serve any prison sentence. And, they argued that it does not even come close to being severe enough to prevent him from being extradited. But lawyers representing Assange argued the assurances over his future treatment were 'meaningless' and 'vague.'

It was on October 2021, when the appeal hearing began in the British high court. Assange did not attend due to poor health. But he later appeared from a video link in prison. Lawyers representing the US argued that Assange's health issues were not as severe as his legal team had claimed during the initial extradition hearing. In the previous proceedings, Assange's psychiatrist had failed to disclose Assange's relationship with Stella Moris, a lawyer originally on his legal team, and the couple's two children, who were conceived during Assange's stay in the embassy. Having the responsibility of children lowered Assange's likelihood of suicide, US lawyers argued. They also pointed to the lower rate of suicides in prisons in the US compared to the UK and argued that Assange's depression was 'moderate' rather than 'severe.'

In Assange's defence, his lawyers argued that his risk of suicide remained substantial, and defended the psychiatrist's decision not to disclose Assange had a partner and two children.

Representing Assange, Edward Fitzgerald pointed to several revelatory investigations by the press concerning Assange's time in the Ecuadorian embassy. In 2019, the Spanish newspaper El Pais published evidence that a Spanish security firm tasked with protecting the embassy building had been secretly surveillant about Assange, his lawyers, and visitors, and reporting information to the CIA. Security staff allegedly also took samples from a baby's diaper to check whether Assange and Moris were the child's parents. That is why, given the threat of constant surveillance, Assange's psychiatrist withheld Stella Moris's relationship with Assange for safety reasons, Fitzgerald argued in court. Moris went public as Assange's partner in April 2020.

His fiancé, Moris argued that Assange is innocent because the Espionage Act should not be used against publishers of information in the public interest. However, a senior extradition practitioner who spoke to Time on the condition of anonymity did not believe Assange's actions could be considered as journalism. 'Normally, there is a crucial journalistic process of reviewing material and presenting it', the source said. 'But, in Assange's case, there was no filter, no analysis, just: publish'.

International press freedom advocates, including RSF and Amnesty International, however, are defending Assange on the basis that he acted in the public interest, as they believe his leaked documents were an incredible contribution to journalism around the world.

March 6, 2022

16

WAR WEARY SOMALIA

In the fight against extremism, the United States deployed thousands of troops in places like Iraq and Afghanistan, a move that resulted in a crushing failure. But, in places like Somalia, the United States turned to a different playbook. They favoured spies, special operation raids, and drone strikes, instead of troop deployment. The mission was to hunt al-Qaeda fugitives, which later expanded to fighting Al-Shabaab, the most dangerous of al-Qaeda affiliates. Now, with time, this playbook is also failing.

Al-Shabaab has been strongest in Somalia for years. They roam the countryside, bomb cities, run an undercover state, make extortion rackets, and demand parallel taxes, which are at least $120 million a year, by American government estimates.

Al-Shabaab also has had plans to attack the United States, after the arrest of a militant in 2019, who took flying missions in the Philippines, for conducting another 9/11 attack on the United States. It reflects how Washington's policies are only exaggerating the extremist threats on their country.

Biden administration, however, denies that the mission in Somalia has failed. But they are aware of myriad shortcomings, which is forcing them to initiate a new policy, which is necessarily not troop deployment. In fact, the US government has been reluctant to commit troops to Somalia since the notorious 'Black Hawk Down' episode of 1993, a blazing battle depicted in Hollywood movies and books. After that episode, the United States withdrew its troops from Somalia after more than a decade.

Although, in the coming time, Americans eventually turned up in Somalia in very small numbers through covert operatives, intelligence officers, support admins, and diplomats, who bunkered into a windowless embassy in Mogadishu in 2018. However, fearing another debacle, they rarely ventured out.

Outside the American presence, there are African Union peacekeepers that patrol the streets. Although the streets of Mogadishu bear scars of war, many of them decades old, there are trendy cafes, gleaming apartment blocks, and fast, cheap Internet. Piracy, an international problem stemming from Somalia, has by and large vanished. As Lido beach is packed with tourists and locals, due to a recent peace wave, it had become a target of Al-Shabaab in 2020, thereby denying Somalis a chance for prosperity in the longer term, as fear reigns in their lives again.

On the political level, Somalia's fractious political elite is riven by disputes. After the Taliban's victory in Afghanistan, gleeful Al-Shabaab militants distributed sweets, hoping that they too would seize power someday.

When it comes to the CIA, it has a checkered history in Somalia. In the mid-2000s, CIA officers, regularly flew into a remote airstrip outside Mogadishu, carrying suitcases of money for a coalition of warlords, who had promised to help hunt Al-Qaeda. This operation had badly backfired in 2006, when public hostility against these American-paid warlords increased, after public support to an Islamic group, the Islamic Courts Union which swept power briefly. Then, a year later, Al-Shabaab emerged.

For this problem, the CIA returned to Somalia in 2009, establishing a secure airbase at Mogadishu airport, and then they teamed up with the National Intelligence Security Agency, Somalia's spy agency. It was in 2011 when Americans killed Fazul Abdullah Mohammad, an Al-Qaeda leader behind the 1998 bombings of US embassies in Kenya, and Tanzania. At that time, they seized a trove of valuable intelligence, including a plot to bomb the elite British school Eton and London's Ritz hotel. After that, the Somalis handed everything to the CIA. But, the fruits of cooperation soon became controversial, as human rights groups and United Nations investigators accused Somalia's spy agency of torturing detainees and using children as spies. Some detainees even accused the CIA of torture. It was in 2015 when the CIA station chief in Mogadishu pressed for the removal of General Abirahman Turyare, the Somali intelligence chief, accusing him of corruption, and mismanagement. At the heart of his removal was the dispute over the control of Gaashaan, a paramilitary force, officially part of the Somali spy agency, which was led by the CIA since 2009. For tracking down Al-Shabaab operatives, Gaashaan used cell phone technology to hunt their commanders.

Fighting Al-Shabaab has always been enduring for the United States. They were initially a faction of the defeated Islamic Courts Union. Ousted from Mogadishu, they fled to southern Somalia and launched a guerilla war, including bombings and assassinations against Ethiopian leaders.

By 2008, Al Shabaab had become the most radical and powerful armed faction in Somalia, with thousands of recruits. Their leaders condemned what they called American crimes against Muslims across the globe. The US state department designated Al Shabaab as a terrorist organisation in 2008. In 2012, the group pledged allegiance to Al Qaeda.

It now seems clear that Al Shabaab's broad goal is to establish their vision of an Islamic state in Somalia. In areas they control, they have banned music and movies and impose harsh punishments like stoning accused adulterers and amputating the limbs of accused thieves, just like the Taliban. They went on to perpetrate a series of horrific attacks including, in 2017, a truck bombing in central Mogadishu that killed at least 587 people, which was regarded as one of the deadliest extremist acts in modern world history. As Al-Shabaab leaders were killed off and the Danab, an elite, American-trained Somali commando unit, evolved into a powerful anti-Shabab tool, the militants adapted.

Al Shabaab's influence also extends into the heart of Mogadishu, where the group and its supporters have infiltrated parliament, the business community, and the security services. Due to their popularity, Mogadishu residents have frequently travelled by bus to outlying areas, to have disputes settled with Shabaab courts, rather than government courts.

American analysts estimate that Al Shabaab commands anywhere from 5,000 to 10,000 fighters. Their bombs have grown more sophisticated and powerful. The group uses its hold on Mogadishu port to smuggle in large volumes of explosive materials and Chinese-made trigger devices, according to US officials.

To prevent their growth, Americans launched air strikes

against them. They surged in 2017 under the command of Donald Trump. The US military admitted to killing civilians but did not offer any compensation, in contrast to Iraq and Afghanistan where they paid $1.5 million for hundreds of deaths and property damage.

As per an Op-ed in New York Times by Declan Walsh, Eric Schmitt, and Julian Barnes: 'the American aversion to casualties among US personnel has created an unusually high dependence on private contractors. The best known, Bancroft, hires retired soldiers largely from eastern Europe, Africa, and the French Foreign Legion to recruit and train Somali forces. Bancroft's property wing built the fortress-like Mogadishu embassy and leases it to the State Department; a senior official said it is among the most expensive to operate in Africa.'

The Biden administration is currently trying to evaluate the present crises, and is deciding whether to send back some troops there, who were recalled by Trump. However, the critics of the US's foreign policy in Somalia state that Al-Shabaab is principally focusing on east Africa, and their ability to strike the US is overblown. There are also some analysts who state that the US needs to follow a completely new strategy there, including a political settlement with Al-Shabaab, or face a prospect of a forever war with them.

The Western-backed Somali government is ineffectual in comparison, divided by the corrosive clan politics that have crippled international efforts to unify Somalia's security services. The graft is rampant. Transparency International ranks Somalia, along with South Sudan, as the most corrupt in the world. In fact, in April 2021, Somali soldiers angry over the president's stay in power took up key positions across Somalia's capital, with their truck-mounted machine guns. The prime minister, at that time, had called for a ceasefire and emergency meeting. The president had faced growing opposition in Somalia and abroad after the lower house of parliament approved a two-year extension of his mandate and that of the federal government.

Then, in January 2022, there was a deepening rift between Somalia's president and prime minister, which plunged the Horn of Africa country into a political crisis, after the prime minister got suspended. The prime minister, however, had defied the order, describing the president's decision to suspend him as 'outrageous.'

March 9, 2022

17

SOLDIERS FOR SALE

Mercenaries change warfare in profound ways because they commercialise it, and Colombian veterans have become especially sought after for their perceived value and combat experience. Their reputation stems from years of fighting the FARC insurgency, which honed small-unit tactics, jungle warfare, and counterinsurgency skills that foreign employers prize. Many retire early with meagre pensions and limited job prospects, making contractual work abroad enticing; as The Guardian reported, recruiters describe Colombian veterans as 'battle-hardened, disciplined and relatively inexpensive compared to Western contractors,' which helps explain their prominence in global conflict markets. The Middle East has become particularly lucrative, with deployments across Yemen, Libya, Iraq, Afghanistan, and the United Arab Emirates, where wealthy governments and elites are willing to pay for foreign manpower without the domestic political cost attached to deploying their own troops, a dynamic highlighted by The Washington Post in its coverage of outsourced warfare.

It was in 2015 that The New York Times revealed hundreds of Colombian mercenaries had been contracted by the UAE to fight Houthi rebels in Yemen, reporting monthly pay bands of roughly $2,000 to $3,000, with $1,000 bonuses for those sent to the toughest missions, and occasional offers up to $7,000 alongside promises of fast-tracked residency benefits for families, a package designed to undercut Western private military firms while attracting experienced Latin American recruits. The reports explained that the UAE first relied on a private American company connected to Erik Prince, the founder of Blackwater, to set up a force of foreign mercenaries.

As the war in Yemen grew more intense, however, the Emirati authorities took over the programme themselves. This change showed that Abu Dhabi wanted to keep tighter control and assume responsibility directly, even while continuing to use foreign soldiers. Colombian journalists later traced the recruitment chains back home: El Tiempo and its magazine Don Juan documented the role of ID Systems Ltd and Global Enterprises, firms led by former Colombian special operations officers, with Don Juan's Nathalia Hernandez living for nearly a year in Abu Dhabi with one recruit to chronicle how contracts, training and deployment unfolded in practice.

Blackwater's early links to Latin American recruitment were widely covered during the Iraq and Afghanistan wars, and Colombian outlets reported that many recruits were retirees or men under investigation for rights abuses. Don Juan's reporting described some as 'responsible for false positives,' a Colombian term for extrajudicial killings staged as combat deaths, while Semana added that the government remained conspicuously silent after those revelations, underscoring the sensitivity around veteran accountability and foreign contracting. Colombian guns for hire were also reported in Libya's 2011 civil war, with Semana citing deaths both in Yemen's Taiz and during raids on Gaddafi compounds, a reminder that these deployments were not merely static security roles but involved direct exposure to combat risk.

Beyond battlefields, Colombian veterans were recruited

for more menial but still hazardous tasks: guarding oil pipelines, protecting high-rise infrastructure, and private security jobs in Iraq from 2006 onward, with Semana's investigation into a Blackwater-owned Bogota outfit finding that promised $7,000 monthly pay was reduced to roughly $1,000 upon arrival, leaving men locked into six-month contracts at US bases around Baghdad, a pattern of exploitation that echoed broader concerns about opaque contracting and wage theft.

The economics that drive this market are stark. As The New York Times noted, UAE-backed salaries could be eight times higher than Colombian pensions, pulling veterans into a globalised labour market for violence where cost, experience, and deniability trump formal military hierarchies. The 'conflict market' logic in the Middle East also rests on political acceptability: hiring foreigners is less taboo than in Latin America, and it allows governments to outsource both capability and blame, a point The Washington Post made when describing how states can 'disown' contractors if missions go wrong, firing or prosecuting them without the reputational and legal consequences associated with disciplining their own troops. This outsourcing creates a moral dilemma at scale: mercenaries are valued because they are expendable, yet they operate amid weak accountability, blurred chains of command and the fog of proxy warfare, conditions that invite abuse and complicate international humanitarian law.

The human story beneath the market is equally important. Transition programmes for Colombian soldiers frequently falter as years of war leave psychological trauma and erode civilian employability, with El Pais reporting how veterans feel identity loss and social ostracism, facing precarious jobs and pensions that fail to support a dignified life.

That mix of trauma, low pay and limited opportunities makes foreign contracting both tempting and risky: men may gain short-term income but accumulate further scars and legal vulnerability, and their families absorb the consequences of long absences and uncertain protections. The Guardian's coverage of private warfare highlighted how these dynamics are not isolated to Colombia but part of a wider commodification of military labour that stretches from Latin America to Eastern Europe and Africa, creating a class of transnational soldiers whose rights and liabilities are poorly defined.

A comparative lens shows why Colombians became the backbone of certain Gulf programmes but were not the only Latin Americans recruited. The New York Times reported that Emirati recruiters drew from Colombia, Panama, El Salvador and Chile, citing language compatibility, lower costs, and prior US-aligned training as advantages, with Salvadoran and Chilean veterans bringing conventional army experience and Panamanian recruits adding policing and canal security backgrounds. Colombians stood out for counterinsurgency expertise against FARC, which translated into small-unit operations, perimeter security, and urban clearing—skills the UAE sought for Yemen's most demanding missions, as Times reporters described. Meanwhile, Chileans often commanded respect for their professionalisation and training standards, shaped by decades of US cooperation, a point noted by The Washington Post when profiling Latin American contractors in US-linked theatres.

Salvadorans, many with civil war legacies and later gang-violence policing experience, were channelled into static site protection and convoy roles, according to Latin American security correspondents cited by El Tiempo. Panamanians, typically recruited for protective services, were favoured for guard-force roles in rear areas where Spanish-speaking teams could be organised under English-speaking supervisors, a pattern reported across multiple New York Times and regional features.

Yet across these nationalities, the risk-reward balance looked similar: high-risk deployments offered life-changing pay and benefits that were rarely matched at home, but oversight was limited and grievance mechanisms weak. Semana's exposé of wage underpayment in Bogota mapped onto anecdotal reports from Salvadoran and Chilean recruits about contract bait-and-switch tactics, while El Pais chronicled the psychological wear that repeated deployments inflict on families regardless of nationality. The Guardian's analysis of private military companies noted that contractors from different Latin American countries were sometimes stacked into tiered pay scales, with Western teams commanding premium rates and Latin Americans placed below them, an inequity that mirrored broader north-south labour divides and fed resentment inside mixed units.

Strategically, the use of Colombian and other Latin American mercenaries tells us something unsettling about how states manage war today. The Washington Post argued that outsourcing hard missions to foreign veterans allows governments to avoid domestic casualties and legislative scrutiny, while still projecting force abroad; it is a political technology as much as a military one. The New York Times showed that the UAE's move to internalise the programme after its initial private phase reflected a calculation about control and secrecy rather than rejection of mercenaries themselves, a hybrid model that marries state command with private recruitment networks to maintain plausible deniability. For Colombia, meanwhile, the steady outflow of veterans into private warfare highlights structural weaknesses in support systems and accountability: Don Juan and El Tiempo reported official silence in the face of allegations that men implicated in past abuses were being rehired into foreign combat, a gap that risks exporting unresolved domestic traumas into new theatres.

In the end, Colombian mercenaries have become a defining feature of the modern war economy because they sit at the crossroads of supply and demand: a surplus of experienced soldiers at home and a global appetite for cost-effective combat capability abroad. As The New York Times and The Guardian documented, their presence in Yemen, Libya, Iraq, and Afghanistan shows how conflict has been commercialised and how states engineer deniability by contracting violence. The promises of high salaries and expedited residency contrast with frequent exploitation, psychological strain, and legal uncertainty, while comparative cases from Chile, El Salvador and Panama reveal a layered marketplace in which Latin American veterans shoulder risks without commensurate protections.

The Washington Post's warning stands: when governments can disown mercenaries, accountability decays, and the moral lines between state warfare and private enterprise blur—a trend that will persist so long as the economics and politics of outsourced war make it attractive.

March 10, 2022

18

IRAN'S POLITICAL RANCOUR WITH AZERBAIJAN AND TURKEY

A new resistance force has been announced in Azerbaijan by Iran. It is called Huseynyun, a faction like what Iran has endorsed in the past such as Lebanon's Hezbollah, Yemen's Ansar Allah (Houthis), the Fatemiyoun and Zainebiyoun, composed of Shia Afghans and Pakistani fighters. Collectively, these factions are called the 'axis of resistance' to prevent persecution.

There is little known about the group. Although, many analysts believe that it was first formed during the 2016 Syrian conflict. These developments will bring internal political instability inside Azerbaijan. Although, being a Shiite majority, it is largely secular, and does not subscribe to the Iranian form of government, after years of Soviet rule. It is a close ally of Israel as well as Turkey.

In the past too, Tehran tried to export its resistance inside Azerbaijan, but it did not find much success. It was in 1991 when Iran tried to establish the Islamic Party of Azerbaijan (AIP). The party was eventually banned, as it was accused of being covertly funded by Iran with the aim of overthrowing the Azerbaijani government and turning it into an Islamic republic. The party, nevertheless, remained functional for many years, and there was also an arrest of its pivotal leader, Movsum Samadov in 2011. Iranian Revolutionary Guard Council has also been active in Azerbaijan since the early nineties, according to Israel's Meir Amit Intelligence and Terrorism Information

Centre. This was to ensure that Azerbaijan withdraw its secular character, change its pro-Western orientation, and sever ties with Israel.

Some former AIP members also found their way into Azeri Hezbollah, which has existed in the country since 1993. These members once plotted an attack on the US embassy in Baku. Iran's other over aching concern is Israel's growing proximity to Iran's borders via its military and political relations with Azerbaijan.

Azerbaijan and Israel relations have a close set of variables. Baku has strongly benefited from Israel's military technology, particularly drones, during the war with Armenia. Pro-Israel organisations also are a mainstay of Baku's lobbying efforts in Washington, to neutralise the rival Armenian lobby and dodge human rights criticisms. In exchange, Azerbaijan is expected to continue providing a platform for Israel's intelligence activities aimed at Iran.

Iran has also done several military drills on Azerbaijan–Armenia border, after the first anniversary of the Nagorno Karabkh war, but such displays are unsatisfactory to protect Iranian interests and its borders against hostile foreign elements, such as Israeli expansionism. That is another reason they have started funding groups like Huseynyun.

According to Iranian hardliners, the Zangezur corridor, proposed by Azerbaijan to connect the rest of the country with its Nakhchivan enclave via Armenia's southern Syunik region is a gateway for Israel and NATO's direct entry into the Caucasus and, therefore, would violate Armenia's territorial integrity and threaten Iran.

Tensions had also increased between Iran and Turkey when Erdogan recited a poem during his visit to

Azerbaijan, which was met with Iranian displeasure. Tehran accused Erdogan of encouraging separatism and ethnic tensions in Iran as millions of ethnic Azerbaijanis live in northern Iran. President Erdogan's support for pan-Turkism, an ideology espousing the political and cultural integration of Central Asia's Turkic peoples (which include Azerbaijanis and Iranian Azeris), continues to damage relations between Ankara and Tehran. The naval drills conducted by Azerbaijan and Turkey in the Caspian Sea were also perceived by Iran as a threat.

When it comes to Iran's Azeri community, it enjoys numerous historical, linguistic, and cultural ties with Azerbaijan, and it could fall prey to unprecedented state repression. In the past, there were movements calling for an autonomous Azerbaijani province in Iran, like the Khiyabani insurgency of 1920 or the Soviet-backed Azerbaijan People's Government of 1945-1946. They were short-lived and failed to gain popular support, according to political scientist Ramin Ahmadoghlu. Professor Neda Bolourchi argues that the 1980-1988 Iran-Iraq war did not inspire Iranian Azeris, Kurds, Arabs, Zoroastrians, Jews, or Christians to rebel against the infant Islamic Republic. Yet, Tehran's willingness to clamp down on dissenting minority groups cannot be underestimated. In 2018, Amnesty International reported that Iranian security forces arbitrarily detained and tortured activists participating in Azeri Turkic gatherings. Outspoken Azeri Turks who voice concerns about the lack of opportunities to use or learn their own language are routinely stigmatised, mistreated, imprisoned, or subjected to unfair trials. A similar fate may await many more Iranian Azeris if tensions do not dissipate soon.

While in Azerbaijan there has been a resurgence of irredentism inspired by the thought of 'reunifying' the territory of the Republic of Azerbaijan with the northern Iranian provinces largely populated by ethnic Azerbaijanis and known to nationalists as 'southern Azerbaijan,' in Iran a counter-movement also has gained momentum. From this angle, it is Azerbaijan that must be reunified with the 'Iranian motherland' after being forcibly incorporated into the Russian empire in the 19th century. These views have gained fresh prominence in Iran, especially on the level of public discourse. The influential reformist daily Shargh is instrumental in disseminating them.

Also, for the past thirty years, a significant portion of the Iranian border was under the control of Armenian occupiers in Karabakh, it let Iran develop trade with the illegal occupation regime. Reports revealed that Iran profited from the occupation by supplying fuel, food and other materials to separatists and getting benefits in exchange, such as laundering US-sanctioned money through Armenian banks.

Now, things are tending to change following Azerbaijan regaining full control of its Iranian border, including the important connections that were used to allow Iranian trucks to get through to Karabakh. The Second Karabakh War was in fact a triumph for pan-Turkic solidarity.

However, Iranian trucks have continued to carry supplies to Armenian-populated parts of Karabakh via Yerevan, which is currently host to Russian peacekeeping forces. Baku had started charging customs fees for the trucks passing through the Gorus-Gafan road, the only motorway connecting Armenia to Iran. While Tehran officially remained silent on these additional costs, Azerbaijan arrested some drivers for entering Azerbaijan from Armenia illegally. Iran demanded the release of the drivers and lashed out at the supposedly amateur diplomacy by Azerbaijan. It shows how war games and insults have not abated.

As per an article by Abbas Haidari in Atlantic Council: 'It is unclear to what extent the new Ebrahim Raisi government and Supreme National Security Council can formulate a clear defence and security policy in the face of the security challenge with Azerbaijan. However, what is clear is the possibility of an aggressive defence and foreign policy has given that tensions in the Middle East and the Caucasus are much higher.'

March 15, 2022

19

CASAMANCE CONFLICT IN SENEGAL

Senegalese authorities have launched a military offensive against fighters allied to the Movement of Democratic Forces of Casamance, a separatist group in the southern region of the country in March 2022.

According to Senegal's chief of staff, the offensive aimed to destroy all armed gangs, conducting criminal activities in the area, to preserve the integrity of Senegal's territory. Due to this operation, around six thousand people fled, with most of them taking nothing with them.

Alasan Senghore, the secretary-general of the Gambia Red Cross Society, told Voice of America that the latest episode of fighting is one of the worst he has ever seen. It is because the panic of fighting is in the minds of people most of the time. In the past, this organisation has carried out food distribution for displaced people in the Ziguinchor and Bignona departments of Casamance.

Most of the fighting has been taking place near Foni Kansala.

The main objective, however, is to dismantle the bases of the MFDC faction of Salif Sadio. This mission was planned after the death and capture of some Senegalese soldiers, by the MDFC fighters in the border area with Gambia. The captured soldiers were later released by the rebels following negotiations involving the West African regional bloc ECOWAS.

The MFDC was formed in 1982 to fight for independence for Casamance. It has been blamed for sporadic attacks since then. The group finances itself through timber trafficking between Senegal and Gambia. There are eight thousand refugees produced by the conflict who currently live in Gambia. As evidently documented by researchers, the MFDC had enjoyed the support of both Gambia's Yahya Jammeh and some influential elements in the government of Guinea Bissau in the form of arms supply and sanctuary.

Historically, Casamance was a Portuguese colony, while as rest of Gambia was a French colony. The region also has different religious, ethnic, and linguistic traditions. This uniqueness resulted in the reason it became the most dogged sanctuary of the separatists.

When it comes to Senegal's political leaders, Abdoulaye Wade came to power in Senegal in 2000, after nearly three decades of politicking. He espoused a different strategy from that of his predecessor, Abdou Diouf, under whose presidency the conflict erupted. While Abdou Diouf responded with force, Wade, as a rational calculator, responded with pragmatism, by reducing the role Guinea-Bissau and Gambia played in serving as mediators. He saw larger meetings with them as a waste of time and resources.

Wade, who was an adept diplomatist, once asked the UN to deploy its observers on the Guinea-Bissau-Senegal border, because of a regular cross-border skirmish between MFDC fighters and the Senegalese soldiers. This ruffled feathers in Guinea-Bissau, who did not want the UN to intervene.

The separatist movement, at large, had posed a no larger

existential threat to Senegal, as it is one of Africa's more stable democracies. However, the conflict remains a reputational blemish.

The MFDC emerged as an armed separatist movement in 1982, and with violence peaking in the 1990s. According to UN estimates, the fighting has killed over five thousand people, internally displaced over sixty thousand people, and sent tens of thousands into refuge in neighbouring Guinea-Bissau and Gambia.

Due to this, the Casamance region continues to experience periodic surges of violence as MFDC rebels, whose ranks are estimated at between twelve hundred to two thousand fighters. They commit theft, and engage in drug trafficking operations, through trade with China.

Women, surprisingly, have played a significant role in supporting the move for independence in Casamance. Research has shown that the role of women in armed conflicts has always been underreported. But, in Casamance, the MFDC could not have endured for so long without the women's support.

Casamance could give several economic benefits to Senegal in the longer term if resources are exploited. According to David Seyferth who wrote an article for Atlantic Council, Casamance is blessed with Senegal's most fertile lands, and if the area is cleared of the landmines and other artillery the land could be used to grow fruit, vegetables, and rice.

Likewise, the region's white sand beaches were once a pivotal tourist destination that drew fifty thousand visitors a year. Therefore, peace is only possible if the conflict is resolved. The absence of peace, in fact, prevented the

Senegalese government from taking a larger peacekeeping role in West Africa.

It was in 1990 when Amnesty International first released a report which narrated widespread human rights violations of Casamancais by the Senegalese government.

However, the turning point of the conflict was in 1992 when MFDC split into two factions: Front Sud (southern front led by Abbe Diamacoune) which became primarily a Diola organisation demanding independence, and Front Nord (northern front, led by Sidy Badji) which was organised as an alliance of several groups (both Diolas and non-Diolas) calling for further negotiation based on the 1991 agreement instead of full independence. The main reason for the split was attributed to the Nord people's fear of losing their cultural identity by being dominated by Diolas. Although Front Nord supporters shared the basic objective (greater political, cultural, and economic rights of the Casamance) with the Front Sud, they feared that Diola predominance of the Front Sud could cause the loss of multi-cultural identity among the Casamance people.

On various occasions, the MFDC have admitted that they wanted to create a Gabou federation including Gambia, Casamance, and Guinea Bissau.

There have been ceasefire agreements, nevertheless, between the government and the rebels. Quite recently, it was in 2014, the government led by Micky Sall mandated the Centre for Humanitarian Dialogue (HD) to re-launch negotiations with three of the Southern Front movements, as negotiations were previously interrupted in 2013. The agreement included government concessions including dropping charges against key rebel leaders and promises to promote economic development and political integration of the Casamance region. But, promises of political resolution and economic incentives have not borne fruit till now.

March 20, 2022

20

MOROCCO'S DISSENT AND SUBJECTION

To mark the eleventh anniversary of the 20 February Movement, thousands of activists rallied in more than fifty cities in Morocco in February 2022. They wanted the release of journalists and activists. Waving black flags, they chanted slogans praising the people, instead of the king.

In an interview with New Arab, Alali Aitaoui, a prominent activist in the 20 February Movement believed that none of the legitimate demands first raised by the people in 2011 has been fulfilled.

The brutal phase of repression testified itself after the arrest of prominent activist, Noureddine Al Awaj. He was convicted in 2020 with a two-year sentence for insulting constitutional provisions after saying in an interview that Morocco became a 'disaster' due to failed policies of the regime.

Morocco's Spring started in 2011 after it imitated other Arab nations. The revolution sustained for more than five months. The protests brought together a myriad of political factions, including the secular left, independents and youth from Morocco's largest Islamist association, the Justice, and Charity Group, which is officially banned by the Moroccan monarchy.

The aspiring demands divided the movement between those who insisted that no real revolution was possible without removing 'the king's sanctity,' and those who believed that the movement had reached its goals after the palace's reforms.

The success of the Islamist Justice and Development (PJD) party in the November 2011 elections relieved tensions on the streets. Morocco was in euphoria because it believed that the election was a step towards freedom and democracy.

Despite not officially joining the protests, the PJD had charmed working-class voters with its religious principles and its sharp criticism of classism in the country.

Under the 2011 constitution, King Mohamed appointed the PJD's leader, Abdellillah Benkirane, a palace outsider known for his 'humour', 'tie-less wardrobe', and his promises to end corruption, as the prime minister.

However, the new Moroccan leader quickly became a controversial leader. With a vague posturing, he blamed his cabinet members as 'crocodiles' and 'demons' because there were some shortcomings.

Despite this, his party won the national, municipal, and local elections in 2016 second time in a row. But there was an eventual decline of the party mainly due to its inability to form political alliances, resulting in a political blockage. This led King Mohammed VI to remove Benkirane and appoint Saad Othmani, another PJD member as prime minister.

Under the leadership of El Othmani, Morocco experienced a critical period marked by political instability, economic decline, and a crackdown on dissent.

In 2016, the Hirak Rif movement was also born, when Mouhcine Fikri, a fishmonger in the Rif region, was crushed to death inside a garbage truck after he climbed in to retrieve his shipment of fish that was confiscated by authorities.

The video of Fikri's death, with a male voice in the background saying 'crush him,' fuelled outrage online. The incident spiralled into widespread protests across cities in the often-neglected mountainous region of northwestern Morocco.

As the protests escalated, in May 2017, the PJD and other governing parties issued a statement condemning the Hirak, accusing it of secession and receiving foreign funding. The government then recruited religious officials to condemn the movement.

Authorities had launched a campaign of mass arrests, including the arrest of the movement's leader Nasser Zefzafi.

According to activists' estimates, eight detainees from the Hirak remain in Moroccan prisons to this day, most notably Nasser Zefzafi and Nabil Ahamjik, who are both sentenced to 20 years for 'serving a separatist agenda and conspiring to harm state security.'

In the aftermath of the movement, journalists covering its stories became targets. Claiming the arrests have nothing to do with their professions, Moroccan forces imprisoned three Moroccan journalists namely Taufik Bouachrine, Omar Radi and Soulimane Raissouni, by accusing them of sexual assault. However, the United Nations Working Group on Arbitrary Detention says the cases were politically motivated.

In 2021, an investigation by Forbidden Stories, a network of journalists dedicated to defending reporters and fighting censorship, listed Moroccan authorities among the regimes using the infamous Israeli Pegasus spyware to keep an eye on their rivals. However, the Moroccan government called these stories false and unfounded.

In the September 2021 elections, Moroccan billionaire Aziz Akhannouch's National Rally of Independents (RNI) party won with a landslide, putting an end to Islamist rule in the Kingdom. Although, after less than 200 days in power, the billionaire has already become the target of frustrations.

During the reignition of the 20 February movement in February 2022, the most notable incident happened when citizens stormed a market in the village of Wlad Jelloul, seizing produce and meat in a move of rebellion against the rising costs of living.

Some Moroccans are now accusing the prime minister, who owns Afriquia Gaz, one of the biggest fuel distribution companies in Morocco, of benefiting personally from the fuel price crisis.

According to local analysts, the combination of social struggles and the lack of confidence in the political institutions ruling the country may give birth to a new reform movement.

April 4, 2022

21

COLD WAR BETWEEN ALGERIA AND MOROCCO

It was in December 2020 when Donald Trump ended US neutrality in Western Sahara Conflict. Trump had announced Morocco's sovereignty over every inch of the Western Sahara territory in exchange for Rabat entering the Abraham Accords. It made Morocco the fourth Arab country to normalise relations with Israel in 2020.

Trump's decision violated international law, and the UN's peacekeeping efforts to end the conflict. But, all of this has been traumatic for Algeria. It has led many Algerians angry and extremely worried about national security, as they think Rabat may become militarily superior to Algiers in the future, due to enhanced cooperation between the United States and Morocco.

As Biden has not reversed Trump's decision, it has led to a new cold war between Algeria and Morocco. That is why Algeria severed ties with Morocco in August 2021. While the step undertaken by Algeria may not reflect the same severity of 1994, when Algeria closed its land border with Morocco, following the latter's decision to impose visas on Algerian nationals, due to an extremist attack, it appears to be the final nail in the coffin for hopes of a unified Maghreb, and in the revival of the long-defunct Arab Maghreb Union.

Before 1994, there were broken relations between the two countries as well. The rifts between the neighbours, span back all the way back to the Sand War in 1963.

Then, in 1976, Morocco severed ties following Algeria's recognition of the Sahrawi Arab Democratic Republic (SADR). Relations were then restored in 1988.

There were other factors that came into play in their deteriorating relations since 2021. One of them was Morocco's sponsoring of the Movement for Self-determination of Kabylie (MAK), a separatist group inside Algeria, which was also responsible for deadly forest fires in the country in 2021.

Some commentators argue that Algeria is simply focusing on Israel/Palestine, and the Western Sahara conflict to distract its citizens from domestic challenges. But it has some genuine and practical reasons for opposing normalisation with Israel. In fact, there is an actual risk of Israeli submarines floating around or near Algerian territorial waters. The Israelis, on the other hand, accuse Algeria, without providing any evidence, of working closely with Iran to engage in deleterious activities in the area.

As per an article in Middle East Institute by Zine Labidine Ghebouli: 'Both at the official and popular levels, Algerians are exploring the limits of their relationship with the Moroccans, and this is part of a broader national process of reshaping Algeria's political system and society. This is a process that will determine the future, and limits of cooperation in North Africa. While the pursuit of regional supremacy is concerning, this competition does not necessarily have to lead to open conflict.'

However, since Morocco joined the Abraham Accords, there has been a steady deterioration on the ground in Western Sahara. Today, violence is re-escalating in Western Sahara with the Moroccan military attacking Polisario (Sahrawi) positions. It has made many observers of the Maghreb concerned about a new all-out war erupting between the North African kingdom and the Algerian-sponsored Sahrawi separatist group.

After twenty-five years, the Maghreb Europe Gas pipeline (GME) also has had its operations suspended, due to the growing political tussle. Algiers will now deliver its natural gas to Spain exclusively through an undersea pipeline to avoid going through Morocco.

There is also a certain international isolation for Algeria. Among the most powerful Western powers, there is absolutely no sympathy for Algeria's position.

Turkey, Egypt, and the GCC states, meanwhile, are on Rabat's side, highlighted by the sale of Turkish drones to Rabat and numerous Arab states opening, or planning to open, consulates in Western Sahara.

It is only Russia, which gives Algeria some political sympathy. Moscow sells weapons to Algeria in large quantities. However, Putin will certainly take a side with Morocco, in relation to Western Sahara, thereby not harming its relations with Morocco.

China, which recently sold Algeria drones, might be the power most likely to conduct diplomacy in North Africa in ways that are favourable to Algerian interests and positions. But, like Russia, China has a growing economic partnership with Morocco, which is valuable to Beijing for investment, trade, and other key reasons, giving Algeria more geo-political headaches.

The most surprising fact in this cold war emerged when press stories were out where Rabat was accused of using Israeli Pegasus spyware, targeting over six thousand phones of Algerian politicians, soldiers, members of intelligence services, senior officials, diplomats, and political activists.

The recent escalations between Algeria and Morocco are only diplomatic, and they have not harmed economic relations. At the same time, economic fallout between the two nations will not impact global trade, as intra-Maghreb trade relations barely exceed four per cent of global trade.

April 6, 2022

22

POLITICAL DOWNFALL OF IMRAN KHAN

The demise of Imran Khan as prime minister was a result of an intra-elite struggle after a no-confidence vote was passed in the parliament in April 2022. It was not based on mass people mobilisation, as seen in the late 1960s, and 1980s, or more recently in 2007-08. As 'electable leaders' switched sides in the parliament, his opponents got newer reasons to find flagrant faults in his so-called 'hybrid regime,' which include enforced disappearances of activists, the vicious restrictions on media freedom, the convictions and harassment of political opponents, and the wide, cordial space given to religious extremists.

As per Azeem Ibrahim's article in Foreign Policy, some of Khan's allies even controversially allege that 'the intra-elite struggle' in the parliament was initiated by the Pakistani military, as his government was insufficiently respectful towards China's interests in the country, including audits of some CPEC projects, that angered Chinese officials and Pakistan's military aligned business elite. Historically, the military had cuddled up to Khan in beginning in the early 2010s, first using him and his party, Pakistan Tehreek-e-Insaf (PTI), to pressure the governments of the Pakistan People's Party (PPP) and the Pakistan Muslim League-Nawaz (PML-N) from the street and later, in 2018, installing him in power. Derisively, the PTI's social base, primarily composed of the urban middle class and elite, has historically supported the military's interventions in politics.

Khan is also the latest in a long line of Pakistani prime ministers who have fallen out with the military over key appointments and foreign policy. In October 2021, simmering civil-military tensions exploded in public view when Khan tried to retain Lieutenant-General Faiz Hameed as the military spy chief. Imran Khan had rejected General Bajwa's nominee, Lieutenant-General Nadeem Anjum, who was eventually appointed as the new director general of Inter-Services Intelligence, but the weeklong turmoil turned ominous.

In Pakistan's past, the songs of the military are played in such a way that they want to do business with people with shared interests, as they are threatened by a popular alternative. With time a tussle ensued, the military won, and the civilian government was deposed.

Imran Khan, the self-styled 'anti politician' is back in the political wilderness now. He seems to be abandoned by his coalition allies and has had an impetus to do untraditional things, which will make his encore to power not easy. He tried to be mercurial, had shunned his idealism, but his populism turned out to be his vulnerability, too. Also, he could not nurture his coalition partners well. Ironically, one of his ex-alliance partners MQM notoriously run protection rackets and armed gangs who rob in public in the region of Karachi. Commenting on the Kashmir issue while staying silent on the oppression of Uyghur Muslims to keep economic interests with China alive also showed his hypocrisy. Over the course of time, Khan also did nothing to dispel clientelism in Pakistan's political arena. Stories of corruption also kept on coming from PTI-controlled areas, hinting at hollow promises by PTI leaders. According to Tariq Ali's article in New Left Review, Khan had given membership to advisers and fixers who were deeply secured in the corrupt system, having previously worked with every other political grouping. They constituted a band of careerists, many affiliated to the army, whose loyalties were liable to shift the moment they felt the change in the air.

His ousting was almost theatrical. Pakistani writer, Mohammed Hanif wrote in a Guardian Op-ed with a dash of sarcasm: 'He turned a banal parliamentary procedure into a nerve racking, edge of the seat thriller. He behaved like a child who realises for the first time that other children have birthdays too. Because he believed that if he was not in charge of the house, he might as well burn it down.' Although political analyst Askari Rizvi believes that Khan is still popular among the Pakistani youth, and if he sells his 'anti-American' sentiment right, he might come back in a big way. His demise, however, also shows how turbulent Pakistani politics is, as no prime minister has completed a full term in the office. Even Imran Khan's worst critics did not anticipate the demise of his political fairy-tale like this.

According to an Op-ed in Dawn by Fahd Hussain: 'The rise of PTI the phenomenon was triggered by the inability of the mainstream parties to evolve into mature organisations willing and able to transform Pakistani society in sync with the aspirations of its people.' But that also does not mean that PTI has not done mistakes. It should redeem itself from them in the forty-three months they ruled Pakistan. Its critics argue that its downfall was rooted in its dysfunctional decision-making, and that is why it got kicked around and whipped due to its own contradictions. Hence, PTI will mirror Pakistani society, both in good ways and bad ways, but what is important for PTI in the future will be to purge leading with the bad example. In fact, that holds true for other major parties as well. In fact, PTI had mustered support from big shots in the establishment, and its rise was a combination of inorganic and organic elements, which led to powerful populist outcomes in the rallies, starting mainly in 2011.

A deepening economic crisis also contributed to his bad times with double-digit inflation dogging much of his tenure. In February 2022, when Imran Khan announced a cut in domestic fuel, and electricity prices despite a global rise, it crippled middle-class dwellers and even resulted in malnutrition. That is why the opposition had gained momentum. The move had piled further pressure on Pakistan's chronic fiscal deficit and balance-of-payment troubles. As of now, apart from hyperinflation, depleting foreign reserves is another problem which Pakistan faces.

Conversely, after meeting Putin to seal trade deals in February 2022, Khan even alleged that there was a US plot to remove him, as a punishment for his Russia trip, and neutral foreign policy. The US state department, however, reacted that there was no truth in such allegations. Although Donald Lu, the US assistant secretary of state for south and central Asian affairs, allegedly warned Khan that there would be consequences if he managed to survive the impending no-confidence motion.

April 15, 2022

23

UK MAKES AN INHUMAN PLAN AGAINST REFUGEES

Boris Johnson, the UK's prime minister, has planned to send asylum seekers off to Rwanda in June 2022. Many see this as a quick fix, 'offshored strategy' to instil otherness, sending a clear message that Tory led UK government is not interested to help distressed people in the name of humanity.

Under this plan, many refugees who enter the UK from 'safe' countries will be sent to Rwanda for processing. Only if their claim succeeds will they be allowed into the UK. Even if this scheme is mainly catered to single men, the move will create a lack of cohesion, as they will not be able to raise children, form relationships, and obtain other important rights. It has inflated their hardship. This is, in fact, a contravention of international law. But UK prime minister believes the other way round.

Conversely, the UK supreme court ruled the Rwanda plan unlawful because asylum seekers would face real risk of ill treatment due to a lack of independent and a fair asylum system.

It was back in December 2020, when the Independent reported that Chris Philip, the then UK parliamentary undersecretary of state and minister for immigration compliance and justice, had 'refused to rule out sending asylum seekers to a remote island or disused oil platforms, or creating a 'giant wave machine' to repel migrant-bearing boats in the English Channel.

The move is expected to cost the British taxpayer £120 million, overlooking the fact that the UK is already facing a cost-of-living crisis. The intended plan of sending migrants away will in fact increase the tax burden.

Even before, to stop migrants from entering the UK, the Tories had paid France to smash smugglers and bought armoured jet skis turning back 'illegal dinghies.' Therefore, the global refugee system is crumbling, and the smugness, or even xenophobia, including of the British politicians is making it happen.

In UK's press, many newspapers supported the idea, too. The Telegraph called it a 'landmark immigration deal'. The Daily Express suggested that it was a 'radical blueprint', to stop thousands of people from making the perilous crossing in small boats. The Mail's headline was provocative. It said: 'Rwanda plan to smash the Channel gangs.' The Mail's columnists also welcomed the idea, suggesting that it could break the business model of human traffickers.

The move had withering criticism as well. Steve Valdez-Symonds, refugee director at Amnesty International UK, said the British government's 'shockingly ill-conceived idea will go far further in inflicting suffering while wasting huge amounts of public money.' The chief executive of the UK-based Refugee Council, Enver Solomon, called it 'dangerous, cruel and inhumane.' The British Red Cross expressed concern that 'the financial and human cost will be considerable'.

It was in April 2022, when Priti Patel called it as world's first immigration partnership, believing that it will set standards for managing migration, and help fix the broken asylum system. Hence, it seems that the ocean has achieved a graveyard status because of the criminalisation of migration pressed by the world's enterprising powers including the UK.

What also is ironic is that the UK has proposed a 'business model' to a country, which it blamed for alleged killings, disappearances, and torture.

According to Sally Hayden's article in CNN, part of the UK prime minister's misleading rhetoric is this idea of refugees and asylum-seekers 'jumping the queue.' But there is effectively no queue. In 2021, the British Refugee Council said just 1,587 refugees, most of them Syrians, were resettled to the UK out of more than 26 million refugees globally. According to the UN High Commissioner for Refugees, eighty-six per cent of refugees are currently in developing countries. So, there is no pressure on developed nations to handle the pressure of migrants yet. This perception of migrant overload is mainly concocted by many sections of the right-wing Western media.

The open partnership by the UK with Rwanda has been clearly inspired by contemporary Australian offshore detention activities on the island nation of Nauru as well as Papua New Guinea's Manus Island, which have served as recipes for migrant suicide, self-harm, and general suffering. The move also may be motivated by the United States which has also offered plenty of asylum evicting ideas, as in the case of the Trump administration's so-called 'safe third country agreement' with Guatemala, which enabled the US to deport asylum seekers to a country that was itself not at all safe and a significant source of refugees in the first place. The Tory-led British government may also be inspired by the Trump-era Migrant Protection

Protocols (MPP) programme, re-imposed by Joe Biden, which basically consists of forcing vulnerable migrants to risk their lives waiting in Mexico, another prominent source of refugees, for their asylum claims to be processed in the US. Between 2014 and 2017, thousands of asylum-seekers were also sent to Rwanda from Israel: They later fled or were tricked into crossing into neighbouring Uganda, where they were not granted legal rights. It shows the UK, for these anti-asylum activities, is just another new country on the block. Now, like the UK, Denmark is also vying to send migrants to Rwanda.

April 19, 2022

24

TAKEAWAYS FROM THE NEGEV SUMMIT

For further normalisation of Israel-Arab relations, Negev Summit happened in Israel in March 2022. Organised by Israel's Foreign Minister Yair Lapid, it was a diplomatic move which would strengthen the already drafted Abraham Accords. Four Arab states, including the United Arab Emirates, Bahrain, Morocco, and Egypt attended the summit.

There was a hefty dose of symbolism to the Negev Summit, beginning with its location which was in Kibbutz Sde Boker, the final home of Israel's founding prime minister, David Ben-Gurion, who was also the first signatory of the country's declaration of independence.

The Negev Summit was also concomitant as it took place twenty years to the day since the adoption of the Arab Peace Initiative at the Beirut Arab League summit of 2002. That initiative, ground-breaking at the time, offered full normalisation and peace with Israel upon Israel's acceptance of a Palestinian state and the fruition of a two-state solution.

The summit gained international prominence due to the presence of the US Secretary of State, Antony Blinken. The threat of Iran and the Palestinian matter was discussed, although the Palestinian issue fell to the bottom of the agenda, with only a few participants raising their voices for a solution. This seemed in lieu of the abandonment of Palestine by many Arab states.

Due to Abraham Accords, Israel has continued to expand its settlements in the occupied West Bank and East Jerusalem. This summit gave another reason for Israel to widen its regional acceptance.

Surprisingly, Arab countries did not mention the Amnesty International and United Nations Human Rights Council report which has concluded that Israel is guilty of apartheid against Palestinians and crimes such as torture and collective punishment. The siege of the Gaza Strip and the economic suffering of the Gazans were also not discussed as well. It seems that occupation has become Israel's trademark.

The late addition of Egypt to the summit also represents a major step forward in its normalisation with Israel. Israel and Egypt have maintained a cold peace since signing their original historic agreement in 1979. That peace agreement, however, was nearly in tatters when long-time Egyptian President Hosni Mubarak was replaced by Mohammad Morsi of the Muslim Brotherhood, and several of its clauses were quickly violated. It was not until the takeover by current President Abdel Fattah el-Sisi that the cold peace was re-established.

The Jordanian government was apparently invited to the summit but declined to attend, citing scheduling conflicts with its foreign minister. But, as the Negev Summit was underway, Jordan's King Abdullah II met with Palestinian President Mahmoud Abbas in Ramallah, signalling Jordan's frustration with the politics of side-lining Palestine in regional diplomacy at the summit. Saudi

Arabia, at the same time, did not attend.

About Iran, the mutual fear driving the participants was the possibility that the Vienna negotiations will result in a new nuclear deal with Iran. The terms of the deal may include lifting all sanctions, recognition of Iran's regional role, releasing an estimated $100 billion in frozen Iranian assets with compensation of up to $200 billion, and significantly, the removal of Iran's Islamic Revolutionary Guard Corps (IRGC) from the US foreign terrorist organisation list.

These potential developments are viewed as disheartening by members at the summit, who have voiced opposition to what they perceive as American softness. Thus, the summit seems to moderate future US action as well. It is because the US, under the Biden administration, is adamant to pursue JCPOA. If the members at Negev Summit fail in their strategy, the United States may end up giving Iran many more concessions. Middle Eastern countries have even expressed concerns about the Biden administration's shift in focus from the Middle East to Asia.

Israel also hopes that the Biden administration will publicly commit to a military strike on Iran, if it withdraws from negotiations, or if it continues with its nuclear aspirations. However, till now, Washington has been unwilling to make such commitments.

One solution to confronting Iran discussed at the Negev summit was to pursue a NATO-style military alliance between regional opponents of Iran. However, Tel Aviv will likely have difficulty in building this alliance.

As per an article by Amr Hamzawy in Carnegie Endowment for International Peace: 'Arab participants in the Negev Summit have come to see Israel in several ways: as a potential ally in regional security arrangements geared toward containing existing conflicts against the backdrop of a waning US regional role; as a partner in prioritising the development of strong economic, trade, and technological ties; and a combination of both objectives.'

The summit's only major takeaway was confirmation at the summit to explore a future in which Washington is no longer the ultimate guarantor of security, and no longer the only recognised superpower in the Middle East.

April 22, 2022

25

AN OBNOXIOUS DISPLAY OF RELIGIOUS FREEDOM IN SWEDEN

Swedish cities of Norrkoping and Linkoping have been rocked by anti-migrant rallies and clashes as Sweden's far-right extremists have gone as far as instigating a campaign for burning the Muslim holy book, the Quran. The riots sparked after an anti-Muslim Danish Swedish politician called Rasmus Paludan, belonging to *Stram Kurs* (Hardline) party, announced his 'burning tour' of the Quran during the holy month of Ramadhan across Sweden in April 2022. The Swedish authorities publicly sanctioned this highly provocative incitement. After that, several other cities witnessed riots as well.

In fact, Azra Muranovic, deputy chair of the Municipal Council of Vernamo and a Social Democrat party politician believed that the Quran burning was a planned campaign. But the Swedish government believes that there are some foreign actors behind the riots, despite giving Paludan a green signal for Quran burning. The local police, however, believe that people have a constitutional right to express opinions, as there is no prohibition for blasphemy in Swede law. The government also alleges that there seems to be some disinformation campaign about Swedish social service agencies allegedly kidnapping Muslim children.

After the incident, Swedish national broadcaster SVT has even dismissed one of its correspondents over comments criticising Paludan following riots over alleged Quran burnings. This is a grave concern as no public condemnation for anti-Muslim sentiment in Sweden by the ruling government has been given yet. In fact, the government seems to run away from responsibly instilling peace and pluralism. They have also not predicted the global spillover of condemnations on such nasty incidents, which might propel in the same way, by sustaining itself firmly, as happened with the Danish cartoon controversy on Prophet Muhammad.

Outside Sweden, there were some international reactions to it. Turkey, Saudi Arabia, Iraq, Qatar, Jordan, and Iran condemned the incident. The Organisation of Islamic Cooperation (OIC) and the Muslim World League also criticised the incident and expressed concerns about extremism, counter-extremism, and Islamophobia.

This is also not the first time Paludan has incited and hurt Muslim beliefs. In 2020, his supporters set cars on fire and stores were damaged in Malmo. He wanted to burn the Quran at that time too and was arrested in France and deported. That same year, Paludan was jailed in Denmark for a month for a string of offences, including racism. He was also banned to enter Belgium for one year. It was also alleged that in 2021 he had written sexually explicit messages to underage boys online.

Chaos erupted almost everywhere Paludan went. In neighbourhood after neighbourhood, police were pelted with rocks by furious rioters. 'We have seen violent riots before. But this is something else,' Chief of Police Anders Thornberg explained in a public statement. 'It is a matter of gross violence against life and property, especially against police officers.' On television two days later, he described a widespread sense among police officers that one did not know 'if you will return home after work, if you will be alive or not when the shift is over and you are met by merciless violence from several hundred.'

Many of the rioters were young men, often second-generation immigrants, from Middle Eastern, North African, or South Asian backgrounds. These individuals often live in economically disadvantaged areas, which are sometimes referred to in Sweden as *utsatta områden* (vulnerable areas), such as Rinkeby in Stockholm, Rosengård in Malmo, and Kronogarden in Trollhättan.

According to the police authority, many of the counter-rioters are involved in criminal gangs. These are the very same gangs that already terrorise their neighbours and compete with the state and local authorities for control of so-called Sweden's 'vulnerable' immigrant areas.

What is strange is that Sweden has seen street riots before, as the country has witnessed attacks on police and rescue workers. But what played out this Easter weekend has left Swedes in shock. It is because this time around, it is not only men on the streets.

As per an article written by Paulina Neuding on Spectator, the weird thing is that even women aged 40 to 60 threw rocks at the police.

Just like the Hardline party, Swedish Democrats are a right-wing populist party that could manage a huge chunk of vote share in the next election, according to a report by Bloomberg in May 2021.

Sweden's neighbour, Denmark knows how serious the situation has become. Denmark recently cited Swedish gang crime and the risk of extremist attacks when it decided to extend its temporary border controls to Sweden. It is an extraordinary decision because the two countries have been in a passport union since 1952.

Neuding further wrote about the aftermath of the unrest: 'Sweden's descent into social unrest is a remarkable development in what was once one of Europe's most stable societies. It is a development that other western countries would be wise to watch very closely, in order not to repeat the same mistakes.'

April 24, 2022

26

SECURITISATION OF EUROPEAN AND AMERICAN BORDERS

By tightening national and security protocols, Greece is using Middle Eastern and South Asian refugees to carry out extrajudicial deportations. In a report by Human Rights Watch in April 2022, asylum seekers who crossed the Greco-Turkish border were stripped, beaten, robbed, and forced to wade through chest-high freezing water back to Turkey. This is a sadistic twist on the European border regime. Known as refugee commandos, they work not on money, but on the promises of asylum.

No one should be surprised that the securitisation of Europe's border has directly depended on the violence and humiliation of refugees. Since the Arab Spring happened, the European Union has shaped its border policy in such a way that it deflects people seeking safety inside Europe. No European leader condemns this. Member states are banding together their border defence forces which are now stronger than Frontex, the EU's own border agency.

The right-wing government in Greece has also answered Ursula Von der Leyen's call to act as 'the shield of Europe.' It accuses journalists and NGOs of spreading fake news when they reveal the human cost of halting refugee arrivals.

While on the Evros land border, refugees are tortured and sent back across the river, in the Aegean Sea crossing, the coast guard systemically pushes back refugees by shooting at them and puncturing their boats.

There was also an infamous footage broadcasted in the press in June 2021. Filmed on Croatian soil, armed men wearing balaclavas can be seen beating Afghan and Pakistani asylum-seeking men with batons, forcing them into the river Korana to Bosnia and Herzegovina. Analysis of the footage reveals that the masked men were equipped, and had uniforms consistent with the Croatian riot police, which receive funding from the EU to assist with border security.

Separate footage from Romania even showed border guards undertaking pushback operations at the border with Serbia. The investigation gathered testimony from men and women who were caught up in these pushbacks, testifying that they had been violently assaulted during the same operation.

Traditionally, the EU has paid others to commit human rights violations to keep 'fortress Europe' in order. In the central Mediterranean, the 2017 Italy-Libya agreement used EU funding to transform Libyan militias into coast guards, holding back refugees trying to reach Italy.

In the Aegean, the 2016 EU Turkey agreement ensured that refugees attempting the passage to Greece were intercepted and returned to Turkey by Turkish border forces. While these agreements came at an immense financial cost, they had the benefit of keeping both the EU's territorial integrity and its 'European values' intact.

In 2020, Turkey threatened to stand down as Europe's border protector. It thus created a dangerous gamble in vesting its faith, political reputation, and financial resources as a third-party custodian of Europe's borders.

According to an article by Chloe Haralambous in The New Arab: 'Turkey's periodic belligerence has dispelled Europe's colonial illusion that it can count on the continued obedience of its neighbouring countries, and today it falls increasingly on the EU's own member-states to do the dirty work necessary for vouchsafing Fortress Europe.'

No official record exists of the thousands of people who made it to Europe and were illegally sent back. This is, in fact, a grave inhuman strategy on brown people, as the invention of these squads speaks of a certain sadistic mindset. The brown people are bad immigrants who are ought to be despised, according to many Europeans.

Although, in the aftermath of the Ukrainian war, the securitisation of the European border debate has come under the limelight. It is because the Europeans are welcoming white refugees, even their pets are given preferential treatment over blacks, thereby criminalising non-white refugees seeking the same protections. It is also a direct violation of United Nations conventions, as anyone fleeing war has an equal right to safe passage, regardless of nationality, skin, and colour.

Unlike Ukrainian refugees, who have been taken on board even by President Joe Biden, non-white refugees are met with hostility and a shameful lack of empathy. They were also not offered a fast-track way to legal status, education, or the job market, unlike Ukrainian refugees.

This stance by Biden is also shameful, much like his European counterparts, because he sent back Haitians to their country, who were fleeing a natural disaster and political turmoil. Among all the denialism and political obfuscation in our chaotic world, the simple fact is that there is a much greater value placed on the lives of white refugees.

April 30, 2022

27

TURKISH ATTACKS IN PKK DOMINANT AREAS

In a calculated manner, Turkey launched its new cross-border operation, codenamed Claw Lock against Kurdistan Workers Party in northern Iraq in April 2022. Post-2015, it is Turkey's latest effort to strangle PKK's freedom of movement, and gradually weaken its associates.

Operation Claw-Lock is the successor of the similarly named joint air and ground operations Claw-Lightning and Claw-Thunderbolt in 2021, and Claw-Eagle and Claw-Tiger in 2020.

The Turkish military is carrying out helicopter-borne commando raids on mountains and into caves. Unlike past operations that concluded by winter, Turkish forces, in these new operations, are making gains all year round, through the establishment of an increasing number of military outposts, and forward operating bases in strategically important areas.

Although these operations have failed to rout out PKK in the Qandil stronghold, they have nevertheless put unprecedented pressure on the group.

Turkey is also alleged to have used chemical weapons in its campaigns against the Kurdish Workers Party (PKK) at least '164 times', according to Zagros Hiwa, a spokesperson of the Union of Communities of Kurdistan (KCK).

It was in July 2015 when the ceasefire between Turkey and PKK completely collapsed. The ceasefire first happened in 2013. Then, in 2016, Turkey's Kurdish-majority southeast experienced levels of violence not seen since the 1990s. The PKK fought against the Turkish security forces in urban centres. It made Turkey impose punishing long curfews in entire city districts, and large swathes of Kurdish-majority towns and cities were reduced to a heap of debris.

In May 2021, Iraqi Kurds also expressed their frustration when satellite images revealed that Turkey was deforesting the Iraqi Kurdistan border with Turkey. The aim had been to build roads for military posts. With time, Turkey has established at least forty military bases and outposts throughout the autonomous Iraqi Kurdish region as part of this effort.

Kurdish analyst Ceng Sagnic recently pointed out that the conflict has recently reached 'topographically difficult regions' in the autonomous Kurdish region that has been under undisputed PKK control for over 25 years.

Abdulla Hawez, another Kurdish analyst, noted that Turkish positions along the border suggest that the Turkish army is gradually creating what appears to be a belt throughout its border with Iraq. Such a 'belt', most of it, would undoubtedly constrain PKK movements between Iraqi Kurdistan, Turkey and possibly Syria as well.

After the launch of Claw-Lightning and Thunderbolt, Turkey's interior ministry announced that the military would establish a new base in Iraqi Kurdistan's Metina region. The very next day, the Turkish minister of defence made an unscheduled visit to Turkish troops based in Iraqi Kurdistan, briefly raising eyebrows in Baghdad.

Turkey also opposed the PKK forming what it called a 'terror corridor' across northern Syria. By 2015, the SDF controlled two-thirds of northern Syria's border regions, extending from the Iraqi border in the east to the east bank of the Euphrates River.

There also might be a renewed offensive by Turkey in the Sinjar region of northern Iraq, where IS infamously subjected the Yazidi religious minority to a notorious campaign of genocide beginning in August 2014. The PKK intervened against Islamic State and saved thousands of Yazidis in the process. Turkey then tried to retain its presence there amid operations of Sinjar Protection Units.

It has repeatedly condemned the PKK's presence there for years now, invariably pledging not to allow a 'second Qandil' to be established there. Sinjar is strategically important for the PKK, and its Syrian wing, since it enables its fighters to transit overland from Qandil to northeast Syria.

Shortly after Turkey conquered Afrin, Turkey even upped the pressure against the PKK in Iraqi Kurdistan, beginning a string of extensive air and ground operations that continues to the present day. Dubbed 'Tigris Shield' by Turkish media, it was the most significant Turkish operation in Iraqi Kurdistan since the short-lived Operation Sun in late February 2008, just over a decade earlier. In the following years, Turkey also expanded its networks of bases and outposts, establishing military bases in the mountains of Iraqi Kurdistan's Erbil province for the first time. It also assassinated high-profile opponents such as PKK member Zaki Shingali in Sinjar in an air or drone strike on his convoy.

Turkey, repeatedly, is also using its militia proxies. It uses them to invade a swath of territory between Kobani and Jazira, occupying the cities of Tal Abyad and Ras al-Ain. Turkey stopped its offensive after reaching separate ceasefire negotiations with Russia and the United States but retained its hold of the new areas it had invaded.

By 2020, data showed that 77 per cent of clashes between the Turkish military and the PKK were taking part in Iraq rather than southeast Turkey, the site of the bloody urban battles of 2016. ISIS offensives have also played their part in the war, especially in the region separating the Syrian Kurdish canton of Kobani from the north-western enclave of Afrin.

Turkish Defence Minister Hulusi Akar once said that their operations are based on a strategy that will completely lock the borderline between Iraq and Turkey to the PKK. In other words, it also means that an independent greater socialist Kurdistan, even an autonomous state will leave Erdogan uneasy. Thus, he does not want Kurdistan to integrate. By also attacking Hashd Al Shaabi (PMF) a pro-Iranian armed group, Turkey sent a clear message to the Shia factions to remain outside of Turkey's political game in Iraq.

May 8, 2022

28

THE DOCTRINES OF MACRON

Emmanuel Macron's re-election in April 2022 marked an important moment in contemporary French politics. By securing a second mandate, he became the first French president in two decades to win re-election, the last being Jacques Chirac in 2002. The achievement confirmed that Macron's political experiment launched only a few years earlier with a brand-new movement and without the backing of traditional party structures had transformed the country's political landscape. His presidency has been defined by ambitious reform, an attempt to reshape the centre of French politics, and a controversial mix of liberal economic policies and assertive state authority.

From the moment he first sought the presidency in 2017, Macron presented himself as a reformer determined to break with the old political order. France had long been dominated by the alternating power of the centre right Republicans and the Socialist Party. Macron disrupted this system by founding La Republique En Marche, positioning it as a pro European reformist force that straddled the ideological centre. His success effectively shattered the traditional party alignment that had structured French politics for decades. As political observers noted, Macron's rise created a new political axis in which the centre was occupied by his movement, while opposition increasingly gravitated towards the populist left and the nationalist right.

Domestically, Macron's first term was characterised by significant economic and labour reforms. His government introduced measures designed to liberalise the labour market, encourage investment, and reduce unemployment, which had long been a structural problem in France. Labour regulations were simplified, corporate taxation was reduced, and policies aimed at encouraging entrepreneurship were introduced. These reforms were controversial, particularly among trade unions and sections of the working class who feared the erosion of social protections. Yet the policies also contributed to a measurable improvement in employment figures before the economic shock of the COVID-19 pandemic. By the end of his first term, unemployment had fallen to levels not seen in more than a decade.

His administration also pursued reforms to France's welfare and pension systems, arguing that demographic pressures made change unavoidable. One of the most contentious initiatives was the proposal to raise the retirement age from sixty-two to sixty-four, a measure that Macron argued was necessary to sustain the pension system in the long term. The reform triggered widespread protests and strikes across France, illustrating the enduring tension between economic reform and France's deeply rooted social model. Nevertheless, Macron and his supporters insisted that such changes were essential if France was to remain competitive within the European economy.

Macron's governing style has also been distinctive. The French Fifth Republic created by Charles de Gaulle in 1958 gives substantial executive authority to the president. Macron has used these institutional powers energetically, centralising decision making within the Elysee Palace and cultivating an image of strong presidential leadership. Critics have accused him of governing in an overly technocratic and centralised manner, while supporters argue that decisive leadership has been necessary in an era of political fragmentation and crisis.

Internationally, Macron has sought to project France as an independent and influential power within Europe and beyond. A committed advocate of European integration, he has repeatedly argued for a stronger and more autonomous European Union. In speeches and interviews, he has promoted the idea of European strategic autonomy, urging the EU to reduce its dependence on external powers in defence, technology, and energy. In a widely discussed interview with Der Spiegel, Macron called for a form of heroic politics capable of revitalising Europe's global role.

France's foreign policy under Macron has therefore emphasised both European leadership and diplomatic engagement with global powers. His attempts to maintain dialogue with Vladimir Putin prior to the full-scale invasion of Ukraine in February 2022 were part of this strategy. Macron believed that maintaining channels of communication with Putin might help preserve European stability. Although these efforts ultimately failed to prevent the conflict, they reflected his broader approach of combining diplomacy with European solidarity.

Another major element of Macron's foreign policy has been France's continued military involvement in the Sahel region of Africa. Through operations such as Operation Barkhane, France sought to combat jihadist insurgencies in countries including Mali, Niger, and Burkina Faso. While these missions were initially welcomed by some governments in the region, they gradually became politically controversial. Anti French sentiment grew in several Sahelian states, and France began withdrawing its forces from Mali in 2022 after tensions with the country's military leadership. The episode illustrated the limits of France's traditional role as a security guarantor in parts of Africa.

Migration policy has also been an area of tension and debate during Macron's presidency. France has remained committed to the European Union's collective approach to managing migration across the Mediterranean, which includes cooperation with North African states to reduce irregular crossings. As journalist James Snell argued in The New Arab, the French position that emerged during Macron's years in power suggested that stability along the Mediterranean coast was increasingly seen as essential for managing migration flows. European governments including France have therefore supported regional initiatives such as the Western Mediterranean Forum, also known as the 5 plus 5 Dialogue, which brings together European and North African countries including Algeria, Libya, Mauritania, Morocco, and Tunisia to discuss security, development, and migration.

Yet Macron's approach to migration and integration has often been criticised from multiple directions. Human rights advocates argue that European policies risk prioritising border control over humanitarian obligations, while political opponents on the right accuse the government of failing to curb immigration sufficiently. This tension reflects a broader debate across Europe about how liberal democracies should balance openness, security, and social cohesion.

Perhaps the most sensitive domestic issue confronting Macron has been the question of secularism and the integration of Muslim communities in France. The French principle of *laicite* emphasises a strict separation between religion and the state. In recent years Macron's government introduced legislation aimed at combating what it termed Islamist separatism. The law passed in 2021 as the Law Reinforcing Respect for the Principles of the Republic sought to increase oversight of religious organisations, regulate foreign funding for mosques, and strengthen the state's ability to intervene against extremist networks. Before his first time election, he was pro immigrant which included taking care of war refugees, including putting a moral duty on the French state to give asylum to genuine applicants. Now he is clearly against those policies.

Supporters argued that these measures were necessary to defend the secular republic and prevent radicalisation. Critics however contended that some provisions risked stigmatising ordinary Muslims and expanding state surveillance of religious life. Sociologist Etienne Ollion of the French National Centre for Scientific Research noted in an interview with The New Arab that actions such as dismantling migrant encampments in Calais or tightening regulations on Muslim organisations had sometimes blurred the line between security policy and broader cultural tensions. According to Ollion such policies have occasionally benefited far right narratives by reinforcing fears about immigration and identity.

Indeed, the political environment in which Macron governs remains highly polarised. France's far right has grown steadily stronger over the past decade. Marine Le Pen leader of the National Rally reached the second round of the presidential election in both 2017 and 2022. Other right wing figures including journalist turned politician Eric Zemmour have also pushed the political conversation further towards issues of identity and immigration.

One concept that has increasingly entered political discourse is the so-called great replacement theory. First popularised by the French writer Renaud Camus in his 2011 book *Le Grand Remplacement* the theory alleges that European populations are being deliberately replaced by immigrants from non-European backgrounds. Although widely dismissed by scholars as a racist conspiracy theory the phrase has nonetheless circulated in far-right political rhetoric. Its international notoriety grew after the 2019 Christchurch Mosque attacks in New Zealand where the perpetrator referenced the theory in his manifesto.

In France elements of this discourse have occasionally been echoed by mainstream political figures seeking to appeal to right leaning voters. During the 2022 presidential campaign conservative candidate Valerie Pecresse faced criticism after invoking the term in a speech. Analysts observed that the normalisation of such rhetoric reflected the growing pressure on centre right politicians to compete with the far right for electoral support.

For Macron this evolving political landscape presents a complex challenge. His strategy has often involved occupying the political centre while allowing opposition forces to compete on the ideological extremes. In the short term this approach helped consolidate his electoral base and secure re-election. In the longer term however, it risks further polarising the political system by strengthening both radical left and nationalist movements.

As Macron began his second term his allies suggested that he would adopt a more consultative style of leadership. Whether such a shift can ease political tensions remains uncertain. France today faces multiple pressures including economic adjustment social inequality debates over national identity and the broader geopolitical turbulence reshaping Europe.

Macron's presidency therefore represents both continuity and disruption in French politics. He has modernised aspects of the economy reaffirmed France's commitment to European integration and attempted to project diplomatic influence on the global stage. At the same time his reforms have provoked fierce domestic opposition and exposed deep divisions within French society. Navigating these contradictions will likely define the remainder of his presidency and shape the trajectory of French politics in the years ahead.

May 16, 2022

29

SCOTT MORRISON'S LOSS IN AUSTRALIA

In 2019 when Scott Morrison won an election, he said that he believed in miracles. In the 2022 election, it seems that he ran out of them. After the verdict, he accepted defeat, and believed in the 'judgement of the Australian masses.' Among the two major party leaders, Morrison was looked at as more of an experienced image builder. He projected himself as the typical 'Australian dad,' someone who you can trust, someone who had seen the country through the pandemic, and whose governing Liberal-National coalition had been the better economic manager of Australia.

With time, however, Aussies started disliking him. The image of a trustworthy family man had been eroded over the past three years because they thought that it was not genuine, and not to be trusted. There were many moments in the last three years when his leadership fell short. Many of those affected by Australia's natural disasters believed that he was not on the ground when he needed to be. They also thought that he was there just for photo ops, and was not listening to people's concerns. During the Black Summer bushfires, there were infamous pictures floating around about his vacation in Hawaii. When he eventually went to the fire-ravaged areas, he was heckled by angry locals, and videos of people refusing to shake hands with him went viral. In fact, these images will still haunt him after the election. He was also alleged of sexually assaulting Britney Higgins inside a ministerial office in

Parliament House. It had been a moment of reckoning, hugely embarrassing for the government.

Economically, the Liberal-National coalition was thrown into major curveballs. There had been a rising fuel cost and high cost of living crises. The Reserve Bank had increased interest rates, which was bad news for mortgage owners and first-time buyers. It was also bad news for Morrison's campaign. Even though the economy recovered well, especially during the Covid 19 pandemic, many common Australians were still worried about putting food on the table and making the ends meet.

After the election, pundits noted that democracy can stay healthy even if voters are disgruntled. In Australia, it is the fourth time, after the World War, the Labour Party, this time under Anthony Albanese, had been elected to form the government from the opposition.

Morrison lost not only to Labour but also to a group of female independents who adopted the colour teal, a blend of Liberal blue, (to signal they were economically conservative), and green (to signal they were progressives on climate change and the status of women). The teal independents won seats in wealthy parts of Sydney and Melbourne that had long voted Liberal, including that of Morrison's deputy, Treasurer Josh Frydenberg. The other important factor that came into play was that for years, Morrison's party had failed to run women for winnable seats. Labour also had a better policy on child care this time around.

According to ABC's vote compass, the country's largest survey of voter intentions, a majority of voters also wanted stern action on climate change. That is hardly surprising in a country that has been ravaged by floods and fires of increasing severity. In terms of media support for elections, it is evident now that Rupert Murdoch no longer calls the shorts, in an era of social media campaigns, and multiplying sources of information. In fact, almost all his newspapers editorialised in favour of Morrison.

Richard Glover wrote in Washington Post about the fall of the Liberal Party: 'Labour was like an echidna, the spiky Australian animal that rolls into a ball when attacked. Morrison kept attacking, as if he knew no other mode, even though Labour's small-target strategy gave him so few opportunities.'

Morrison, as a marketing man, also created snappy slogans that went against him in the end. 'I don't hold a hose, mate,' was his answer when questioned about a holiday in Hawaii during the bushfires of the summer of 2019-2020. And, 'it's not a race' was his reply when asked in March 2021 why his government was so slow in ordering vaccines during the pandemic. But, in the end, it turned out that it was a race, and it became clear that Australians wanted a leader willing to hold a hose.

What separated Morrison from Anthony Albanese, the new Australian prime minister is that Albanese was seen someone of a shrewd negotiator and a careful tactician in the campaigns. E.J. Dionne Jr. wrote in his Washington Post Op-ed that he is like an Australian Joe Biden, with a common touch and long experience in the parliament. He made Morrison, an unpopular incumbent, the main issue, in a scenario which eventually resulted in his rise.

May 29, 2022

30

SINAI AND SISI'S REPRESSION IN EGYPT

The attacks in the Sinai Peninsula in May 2022 by the Islamic State were one of the deadliest in the region in recent memory, and they raise an important matter at hand: if Abdel Fattah al-Sisi must be supported by Western patrons for 'counter-terrorism ties', why is Islamic State still successful in expanding extremist activities in Egypt? And, why hasn't he become successful until now?

To combat extremism efforts, the Egyptian military had expanded in the areas of northern Sinai between the Gaza strip in the east and the Suez Canal in the west, allowing for a return of some civilian activity. But the strategy has largely backfired as Islamic State militants are continuing to seek refuge in the desert, and are using different tactics such as sniping and planting explosives.

Sinai, itself, has been brimming in conflict for decades. It started with Naseer's dubious pan Arabism, and Egyptian discrimination against Arab Bedouins, which reduced them to non-citizens. When Sinai began a new era of redevelopment, the former Bedouin villages such as the tiny fishing village of Sharm el-Sheikh, became massive tourist resorts. Even Morsi had a plan for a new Sinai where he wanted legislation to give grassroots land ownership rights to local populations and insisted on a dialogue with local Bedouin leaders. The hope was that the Bedouin residents of the Sinai would reap the rewards of these changes. Instead, in Sisi's time, they were forcibly evicted from their homes to make way for commercial developments by foreign corporations for rich Western tourists.

To add insult to injury, Egyptians from the Nile Valley and Delta were lured in to take up jobs in the booming service industry, putting out local Bedouins from even menial jobs and leaving them destitute. Although the conflict in Sinai precedes Sisi, the Islamic State gained a strong foothold there, after the coup brought him into power. They used the Bedouin struggle to create a ruthless war, especially against Christians and Sufi Muslims, and those who opposed Salafi jihadism.

The election of Morsi, who was a proponent of Islamic democracy, boosted Islamic State's ideological logic as well, as they thought modern democracy and Islam together were heretical.

In Sinai, the Islamic State functions as a racket. For weeks, or years, it fails to make headlines, but then they randomly start attacking and killing civilians, getting back into the limelight. This is then used by Sisi to increase his power of repression in Egypt.

The lack of censure of Egypt by the United States is also letting it fail to address the grave human rights record, which has been never publicly condemned by Washington. US officials, repeatedly, have also concluded that its relationship with Egypt is complex. They have all along wanted a passage of US warships through Suez Canal, and want overflight access to American military aircrafts. Despite its deep ties with the United States, Egypt is also diversifying its source of arms, since Barack Obama in 2013 froze the delivery of some military aid to

Egypt after Morsi's overthrow. Due to this reason, it is now buying arms and ammunition from Russia, France, Italy, and Germany.

The Western leaders, be it, Biden, Macron or Merkel, have typically praised Sisi as a role model for 'stability'. It also proves that they are doing lip service in the name of liberty, and universal human rights back home, as neither could care about the regime's victims. In fact, Merkel in her visit to Egypt in mid-2018 finalised her deal, where Sisi imprisons migrants in the country, to stop them from reaching Europe's shores, in return for lucrative trade deals with Germany and the rest of Europe. It contradicted her stances of the past

In recent times, Sisi has also arrested political workers of the opposition parties such as Strong Egypt Party, a party with Islamist leanings. They were part of 'coalition of hope', who planned to run in the parliamentary election of 2020. However, the critical moment of repression came when Sisi went on to arrest two thousand three hundred people, including the former head of the liberal Constitution Party, and its spokespersons. Curated electoral lists were also devised during the 2020 election, where lion's share of seats was given to the Mostaqbal Watan party, which has had a close connection with state security services. Therefore, neutralising civilian political actors and concentrating power in the hands of the security establishment, to whatever limits necessary, has been the essence of Sisi's ruling junta. This can be further elaborated by the revelations of exiled contractor Mohamed Ali in 2019, who exposed widespread corruption in military-led construction projects: when mass protests broke out against this problem, the protestors were met with sweeping repression. The crackdown on labour activism has also become widespread. In December 2020, heavy prison sentences were slapped against thirty-five residents of Warraq Island, which was an epicentre of clashes in 2017 between local authorities and residents, following attempts by security forces to evict the residents. The mysterious murder of Guilio Regeni, an Italian PhD student, had also created an uproar. The killing was pointed out at the Egyptian state security probably because he was involved in researching about Egypt's independent labour activism.

In Egypt, the heavy reliance on repression is an ideological narrative, essential to maintaining the healthy spirit of the security establishment. With time, this narrative has become difficult to control. According to Sisi, there is an international cooperation between Muslim Brotherhood and other opposition groups, which according to him, are destroying the Egyptian state. Hence, his main justification for the military rule is to protect Egypt from collapse, which can only be achieved through repression, according to Maged Mandour, a political analyst.

Since 2013, the Geneva-based rights group Committee for Justice has also documented the cases of 92 political prisoners who have been executed in Egypt. Death sentences for another 64, which have been upheld by the highest appeals court and ratified by Sisi, could be carried out at any moment. There have been also attempts by Sisi to compel the media to toe the government line. In fact, Egypt ranks 166th out of 180 countries on World Press Freedom Index in 2021.

According to RSF, twenty-two journalists and two citizen reporters are currently behind bars in Egypt. This makes the country 'one of the world's biggest jailers of journalists.' The number of imprisoned media professionals is higher in only three countries: Saudi Arabia, China, and Myanmar.

For many Egyptian activists, the revolution has not materialised and it failed on many fronts. They think they were not better off during the Muslim Brotherhood's brief rule, or during Mubarak's time. For them, the incumbent leader Sisi is a product of the Mubarak regime, and the military, who has led a kind of system, where prison has become a part of their daily life. The anti-protest law discourages them to protest, and there is no progressive space for change. The Egyptian life, for them, in 2022, is like a sad epiphany, where it is difficult to predict where the country is heading to.

May 31, 2022

31

LACK OF GOOD DIPLOMACY ON AEGEAN ISLANDS

Turkish and Greek claims, repeatedly, have overlapped near the Eastern Mediterranean and the islands of the Aegean. Due to this, there is a certain complexity under international law, which is exuberated by a lack of good diplomacy.

For a while, Turkey opposes the militarisation of some islands by Greece. According to Hasan Gogus, former Turkish ambassador to Greece and Austria, Turkey's stance is valid.

According to him, there are several disputes with Greece in the Aegean Sea, such as the width of territorial waters, delimitation of the continental shelf, demilitarisation of islands or length of airspace. While all issues are interrelated, Greece only acknowledges the existence of the continental shelf dispute. Most of the Greek islands in the Aegean Sea are near the Turkish mainland, such as Kastellorizo or Kos. Those islands were given to Greece under the 1947 Paris Peace Treaty on the condition of demilitarisation. However, according to Gogus, Greece violates this provision. But, according to the Greek point of view, Turkey is making claims that are supported neither by the status quo nor by international law.

According to Sotirios Zartaloudis, associate professor, in comparative European politics at the University of Birmingham, the Aegean Sea for Greece is of great geopolitical and strategic importance, as Europe's southeastern frontier to the east and the Middle East along with the Black Sea.

The legal bases of the dispute are found in the treaties of Lausanne (1923), Montreux (1936) and Paris (1947), whereby the treaties signed in Lausanne and Paris regulate which island belongs to which country. However, the treaty of Montreux was intended to replace the treaty of Lausanne partially, and Turkey has essentially been deriving its claims from the latter. Therefore, Ankara's position creates a complex situation concerning sovereign rights in East Aegean, according to Dimitris Papadimitriou, professor of politics at the University of Manchester.

Two years ago, both sides came to a brink of a military conflict, as tensions rose over energy resources in the eastern Mediterranean. Erdogan, in fact, has said that he would not engage in talks until an 'honest Greek politician' was in front of him. Since then, the dispute has spiralled, as he directly threatened war. The response by Greece to it, surprisingly, was muted. At the same time, the Greek foreign ministry published sixteen maps intended to document 'the extent of Turkish revisionism', intended to display Turkish territorial claims from 1923 to the present day.

After Erdogan's rhetoric, Athens would be less likely to demilitarise the islands. Greece argues that any military presence or equipment on the islands is there for training reasons and deterrence, and for self-defence, given the numerous landing activities by Turkey on the west coast, and regular violations of Greek airspace by Turkish fighter jets.

Due to this conundrum, the European Union called upon Turkey to behave constructively. On the other hand,

NATO urged both countries to resolve their dispute over the Aegean Island peacefully. It is because even an accident in the Aegean would result in a full-scale war, and Erdogan can also use this dispute to boost his popularity.

This pattern of confrontation and provocation reached a boiling point in the mid-1990s. In 1995, the Greek parliament ratified the United Nation's Law of the Sea, which, among other provisions, allowed states to declare authority over coastal waters up to a 12-mile radius. Fearing that such a stipulation would limit its access to the Aegean, Turkey was one of a handful of nations to oppose the UN agreement.

Athens' decision to endorse the law led to a fierce rebuke from Ankara, with then-Prime Minister Tansu Ciller declaring that any Greek decision to enforce a 12-mile line of control would be treated as a casus belli. Promises to limit Greece's maritime borders did little to ease relations. When a Turkish freighter ran aground near the uninhabited island of Kardak (called 'Imia' in Greek), various political leaders clashed over the question of which country genuinely possessed authority over the island. With the fate of literally thousands of uninhabited rocks at stake, Turkey and Greece deployed ships and troop detachments in anticipation of war. At the end of January 1996, the Greek government relented after Turkish troops landed on Kardak and hoisted the Turkish flag.

Since 1996, neither Turkey nor Greece has demonstrated a willingness to revise its positions regarding the legal or diplomatic issues that divide the two nations. To this day, Ankara still decries what it sees as Greece's unlawful militarisation of the Aegean islands.

Diplomatically, Greece is moving close to France and United States, aiming to upgrade its military equipment and technology through its contractors. But Greece's strategy is mainly grounded in a dogmatically defensive posture. It may give Erdogan a moment of opportunity to pursue a broad set of revisionist goals.

June 28, 2022

32

LONGSTANDING MARITIME DISPUTE BETWEEN ISRAEL AND LEBANON

Due to the demarcation of land and sea borders, Israel and Lebanon have had long-standing disputes. It was in 2010 when off the coast of northern Israel two gas fields were found, holding as much as 1.7 billion barrels of recoverable oil and 34.5 trillion cubic meters of gas, putting the spotlight on the stretch of the eastern Mediterranean. In October 2020, the US eventually brought Lebanese and Israeli officials to Nakoura, a city in southern Lebanon near Rosh Hanikra for negotiations on the maritime border.

Israel, in the past, had agreed to split the area 58:42 in favour of Lebanon. This concession would have in fact helped Lebanon to start drilling for gas as soon as possible, but it soon went into tatters, when Lebanon sharply increased its demands after four rounds of talks mediated by the United States, increasing the disputed area which include the northern end of Karish natural gas field. At the same time, Israel has said that it will defend Karish, which it has called a strategic asset.

In fact, after the arrival of United Kingdom-based Energean, an oil and gas exploration company, drilling operations have begun close to a disputed maritime zone in the eastern Mediterranean. The vessels have not yet strayed across the maritime boundary, known in Lebanon as 'Line 29'. But oil and gas fields do not respect man-made boundaries, which gives Israel a political advantage over Lebanon.

With time Lebanon quickly asked for urgent US mediation to resolve the spat while Lebanese Hezbollah is watching the situation closely. In fact, Hezbollah will resort to force anytime, if necessary, to protect what it says are Lebanon's fossil fuel rights.

According to an article by Nicolas Blanford in Atlantic Council: 'Sporadic negotiations waxed and waned over the years with no result. Then, in late 2020, Lebanon offered a new interpretation of its maritime boundary. This one cut far to the south of Line 23, adding another 1,430 square kilometres to the Lebanese claim. The new Line 29 retained all the Qana gas field inside Lebanese waters and half of the Karish gas field that Energean was preparing to exploit. Israel rejected Lebanon's 'maximalist claim' and said that it will only negotiate the 860 square kilometre pocket. The US mediation, currently headed by Amos Hochstein, the Joe Biden administration's energy envoy, also has balked at beginning negotiations anew based on Line 29.'

However, Lebanon's veteran political leaders, namely Aoun, acting Prime Minister Najib Mikati, and Parliamentary Speaker Nabih Berri, want to adopt a more cautionary stance, perhaps they want to understand the potential ramifications of approving Line 29. If Line 29 was formally adopted, the US almost certainly would drop its mediation efforts, leaving the dispute in stasis with no resolution on the horizon. In such a case, Israel may not be able to exploit the Karish field for the time being, but it has several other gas and oil deposits to pursue further south. Lebanon would be the economic loser, in such a case.

Hezbollah is leaving it to the Lebanese government to chart a course of action. It has appointed Nawaf Mussawi, a Hezbollah former parliamentarian, to handle negotiations with other political leaders, suggesting it seeks a consensual approach. It likely wants to wait before taking any military action. There are few options available to Hezbollah though which would allow it to flex its martial capabilities without triggering an unwanted escalation. One possibility is to deploy unmanned aerial vehicles (UAVs) to the location of the exploratory drilling to circle and film the vessels.

Politically, Israel and Lebanon do not have diplomatic relations and have been in a state of war since Israel's founding in 1948. The countries do not have an agreed-upon land border but are committed to a cease-fire along what is known as the Blue Line, a boundary drawn by the United Nations after Israeli forces withdrew from southern Lebanon in 2000. Add to that, since the ill-fated Israeli invasion of Lebanon in 2006, during which the IDF lost nearly one hundred twenty troops and scores of civilians alongside about two hundred seventy Hezbollah fighters, fifty Lebanese soldiers and police personnel, there has been an understanding between the two enemies that neither would do anything that could spark a return to all-out conflict. Both sides have, until now anyway, recognised a degree of MAD (Mutually Assured Destruction).

US diplomat Hochstein's visit to Beirut in February 2022 and his proposal, which suggests starting Lebanon's negotiations from Line 23 instead of Line 29, might have led Lebanese officials to refrain from amending the decree, for fear of losing Washington's support in other negotiations. At the same time, however, the Lebanese government has yet to give Hochstein an answer regarding his proposal.

If Lebanon resolves the maritime dispute, it could also detach itself from Russian gas, and European Union likely will also help Lebanon with oil exploration investments, and the scenario would boost its economy.

June 28, 2022

33

LIBYA'S POLITICAL STALEMATE

It was in October 2020 when, unpredictably, a ceasefire of sorts, happened inside Libya. It then steered the way for a broad-based political spectrum sponsored by the United Nations in November 2020. The dialogue had managed to appoint a prime minister and a three-member political council, with a planned election in December 2021. However, the election has got delayed due to Haftar's western Libya campaign. There also have been deep disagreements over polls' legal basis, and rival political centres in the east and west of the country.

The disagreements are mainly based on the designation of headquarters, distribution of seats for both chambers, and division of responsibilities between the prime minister, president, cabinet, and local government.

The crises have continued in the form of oil wars, too. There has been an internal blockade which has slashed the output since April 2022. Crude pipelines, refineries, and export terminals have been frequently blockaded by forces loyal to the government, vying for power. The blockade of two major oil export terminals and several oilfields began in April 2022, after the eastern-based parliament appointed a new prime minister in a direct challenge to a Tripoli-based unity government.

In July 2022, there had been a protest at Libya's

parliamentary building in the eastern city of Tobruk, which was mainly demonstrating against poor living conditions and political deadlock. Ever since the war began, Libya has seen punishing power cuts as well, but the scenario is not letting the leaders withdraw their egos from the political scene.

Former Tunisian Prime Minister, Youssef Chahed wrote in an Op-ed for Newsweek: 'Following the 2011 revolution and for far too long, Libya has been used as a tool for destabilisation and a breeding ground for radical ideologues pushing division, violence, and terrorism. The trade routes that once benefited both our countries were essentially cut off. Sadly, aspirations for democratic self-determination in Libya were stymied or squashed against the wishes of the people, fuelling a cycle of hopelessness, distrust, and apathy.'

Several commentators and analysts also state that the Responsibility to Protect (R2P) principle by NATO was not designed to protect Gaddafi's forces from persecuting its own people, but rather there was an ill motive by several countries to steal Libya's oil wealth through it. The BBC has estimated that over thirty thousand Libyans were killed during NATO operations, while Gaddafi's forces killed only around a hundred people. In fact, the suffering that Libyans have endured is beyond description.

When a UN support mission was created in the aftermath of the civil war to help Libyans with a transition in a post-conflict effort, a US diplomat Stephanie Turco Williams was appointed to draw up a roadmap for the constitutional process. When this happened, Abdul Hamid Dbeibeh was elected as head of the caretaker government on February 2021. Williams, in turn, had vowed for safeguarding the sanctity of the election process. As members of the caretaker government had to resign before the December 2021 election, Dbeibeh violated this agreement by remaining in his post. Due to this, the Tobruk government declared the caretaker government invalid, stating that Dbeibeh's mandate had ended. That was another reason the elections in Libya were not held eventually.

However, it made the Tobruk-based House of Representatives organise an election on February 2021, and they chose former Interior Minister Fathi Bashagha as their prime minister. Although, most of the members of the General National Congress did not participate in the election.

As per an article by Yasar Yakis on Arab News, the House of Representatives also claims that Dbeibeh bribed some members of the Libyan Political Dialogue Forum. Whether it is a fact or not, bribery has become common in Libyan politics for a while.

The scenario is also pushing the rivalry between the two factions even more. Dbeibeh's convoy was attacked in Tripoli in February 2022, when the Tobruk parliament was about to convene a meeting to elect a new prime minister. It also seems that Dbeibeh will not give up under these uncertain circumstances. He has expressed interest in a referendum on the constitution, parliamentary elections, and presidential elections.

Both Dbeibeh and Bashagah believe that fair elections are the only way to lead the country out of crises, but each wants the polls to be held by the governments that they are heading. It also seems that Dbeibeh now controls most of Libya's assets.

Stephanie Turco Williams, the US diplomat is now trying

to come up with a solution in Cairo which is acceptable for both sides. It also reflects that Libyan politics needs a strong mediator. However, many common Libyans are also questioning her motives, which involve the establishment of a committee that includes representatives of two competing bodies from Tobruk and Tripoli for a consensual agreement. Many Libyans, contrarily, feel that Williams is biased towards Dbeibeh.

July 22, 2022

34

HUMAN DISPLACEMENT IN WESTERN DARFUR

There has been a wave of killings in the western Darfur region of Sudan, where around one hundred sixty-five people were dead in April 2022. It led to the displacement of a hundred thousand people, which has been a cause of great concern.

The human rights situation in Darfur is ugly and goes back long. Al-Bashir, who has been in prison in Khartoum since he was overthrown in 2019, was indicted more than ten years ago by the International Criminal Court for genocide and crimes against humanity perpetrated in Darfur.

Although attacks in Darfur have intensified since 2019, this time around war spread out beyond communal militias into a wider battle between rebel groups, soldiers, and the paramilitary Rapid Support Forces (RSF).

Amid a global funding crunch for aid agencies, it has been hard for aid workers to alleviate the suffering. According to Jairo Gonzales, deputy operations manager in East Africa for Medecins Sans Frontieres, Sudan is on nobody's radar, as it does not pique the same interest as it used to in the past.

In fact, NGOs working in the region and other parts of Sudan are facing increased taxes and bureaucratic hurdles since the coup, according to various reports by New

Humanitarian.

There was also the withdrawal of the UN-led African Union Darfur peacekeeping mission amid a national political crisis in 2021. According to a report by Philip Kleinfeld in New Humanitarian, 'there was a peace agreement struck in late 2020 in South Sudan's capital, Juba. That deal's signatories include rebel movements from Darfur and other parts of the country.' Although, a peacekeeping force mandated by a 2020 peace agreement has yet to be deployed widely.

Since joining the transitional government in 2021, the Darfuri rebels allied themselves with the military and Hemedti rather than with civilian political parties, whom they considered less powerful and not interested in Sudan's peripheries. But the armed war has continued, sadly.

Some Darfuri rebel groups lacking the means for even basic subsistence have deserted their movements. Also, signatory groups of the Juba deal have also recruited and trained thousands of new fighters, hoping to boost the numbers for absorbing them into the security forces or be given demobilisation windfalls in the future. Although, the Darfuri rebel leaders face pressure from their old operational fighters who returned to Darfur after the Juba deal following mercenary stints in Libya, who expected to be demobilised or merged into state security forces as well. That is why the Sudanese Revolutionary Front, a coalition of rebel groups from Darfur and other regions, is running out of support from its constituents if these attacks keep happening in Darfur.

According to residents and aid workers, the presence of returned rebels in Darfur's urban centres has further militarised the region and increased levels of criminality and banditry.

It is also difficult to conclude who is escalating the recent attacks, and what their real motives are. Residents believe that there are plots to control resources and land, which is polarising the transitional process. Although, some experts believe that the infightings are mainly due to the withdrawal of the UN-led peacekeeping mission, as the transitional authorities failed to fulfil their promise to protect civilians better than the international force. That is why the war could lead the region to its darkest period. It is because a prolonged war could directly impact farmers who would be unable to cultivate, as the agricultural seasons would fail.

While conflict triggers from place to place, there is a clear trend of Arab militias attacking non-Arab civilians – of whom large numbers have been living in camps since the violence of the 2000s. It also seems that the armed Darfuri fighters have divided loyalties, making the war in Darfur even more complex.

In April 2022, the worst violence happened in west Darfur, while the Krcinik attack was one of the deadliest there until yet. Kreinik hospital had received one hundred forty-two bodies. Its residents had fled to camps in main towns and had been surviving on unripe mangoes. Many analysts also conclude that if the Rapid Security Forces and military maintain political power in Khartoum, the Darfur crisis will not improve.

The situation for refugees is also critical in west Darfur's El Geneina, where more than one hundred twenty thousand people are living in overcrowded sites located in government ministries and other municipal buildings.

A local NGO called Coordinating Committee for Refugee and Displacement Camps, also said that the Zamzam refugee camp was encircled by militias, and the Donki Shata area of North Darfur was also attacked. It shows how revengeful and unmerciful the attacking rebel groups are.

There has been more to this recent spate of violence. According to a report by the United Nations Office for the Coordination of Humanitarian Affairs, the violence in Jebel Moon alone has displaced more than 10,000 people, with 2,000 fleeing across the border into Chad. Between January and September 2021, displacement has been about seven times more than during the whole of 2020, constituting the highest number of displacements in at least six years.

July 26, 2022

35

EXILED BRUS OF MIZORAM

It was first in October 2019 when the federal Indian government, alongside state governments of Tripura and Mizoram, began its nine attempt to repatriate more than thirty thousand internally displaced people of the Bru community of Mizoram from six relief camps in north Tripura, where they have been living for almost two decades now. This attempt also led to futility as only a few hundred people returned to Mizoram so far, despite the central government announcing cash doles, and land allocations.

After that, the Indian government tried to settle their issue again. In fact, the federal government, alongside the governments of Tripura and Mizoram, had been trying to repatriate them to their home state over the past decade, but with little success. It is because many Brus cited security concerns and were unhappy with an inadequate rehabilitation package. The first attempt to repatriate the Brus from Tripura was made in November 2009.

The displacement of Brus, also known as Reangs, is one of the most prolonged in post-independence India. In July 2022, New Indian Express reported that the hills of Haduklau, a tribal hamlet in Longterai range of Tripura's Dhalai district are now dotted by small houses for many Brus.

It shows that with time things have changed a bit. Some Brus have agreed in taking land and money to construct the houses, and English medium schools have also been set up for the children as well. The administration had also assured that Antoday cards would be given to them for subsidised ration. A 1,200 square feet plot has been allotted to each rehabilitated Bru family and Rs 1.5 lakh provided by the government to set up a home. The agreement guarantees a fixed deposit of Rs 4 lakh for each family, a monthly sum of Rs 5,000 and a free monthly ration for two years besides setting up of schools in all cluster villages. More than twenty-one thousand people of more than three thousand families are yet to be rehabilitated, who would be given settlement by August 31, 2022. However, how many will agree to go back, only time will tell.

The vexed Bru issue started in September 1997, following demands for a separate autonomous district council for the Brus by carving out areas of western Mizoram adjoining Bangladesh and Tripura. As a result, many Bru people, around forty thousand people, fled from Mizoram to Tripura as ethnic clashes broke out.

During the ethnic clashes, there were verbal duels, between Mizo and Bru groups, and a hitherto unknown Bru militant group, calling itself the Bru National Liberation Front, kidnapped and murdered a Mizo forest department employee in the Dampa Tiger Reserve. The killing led to upheaval, and as a reaction, Bru thatched huts in several villages in Mizoram's western periphery were burnt by enraged Mizo villagers.

Between 1997 and June 2018, Bru representatives signed nine different agreements with the Centre and the state governments of Mizoram and Tripura to ensure the community's repatriation. These efforts were largely unsuccessful.

As per an article by Sanskrita Bharadwaj in Scroll, some leaders in Tripura put forth the suggestion, over the years, of permanently resettling the displaced Brus in Tripura.

Among them was Biplab Kumar Deb, the former chief minister of Tripura, and Pradyot Kishore Debbarma, a scion of Tripura's erstwhile royal family. They both had written letters to the Centre in November 2019. No government organisation, however, has taken up such a discourse. There seems to be a merit in this plan, because a large population of Brus are willing to resettle in Tripura itself rather than have repatriation or relocation to Mizoram. They long to stay in the state, even in exile. Life has made them familiar with the region, which they now saw as their home, despite recent continual government efforts to settle them back in Mizoram.

This, however, does not mean that the Brus should not be alleviated of their poor living conditions in the Tripura camps, because they wish to live there, and not decide to relocate to Mizoram.

The life spent by Brus at the camps is without permanent electricity, and safe drinking water and residents also did not have easy access to healthcare services. Yet, thousands of them have continued to live in camps, for their reasons.

When Sanskrita Bharadwaj travelled to one of Bru camps in Tripura, in Kahamtaipara, 200 km east of Tripura's capital, Agartala, in the Panisagar division of North Tripura district, she found the living conditions appalling and wrote: 'conditions at the camp remain far from suitable for permanent settlement. The road leading up to the location was poorly constructed – a rocky, narrow path uphill. The site did not have water pipelines or a drainage system: most residents, including children, walked down the hill to collect water from a distant stream. The path that led to the stream was unpaved and steep, and residents often ascended barefoot carrying multiple vessels filled with water, work that left them sore and exhausted.'

July 28, 2022

36

AGGRAVATION OF CONFLICT IN ETHIOPIA

July 2022 witnessed Abiy Ahmed, the Ethiopian prime minister, accusing a rebel group of carrying a massacre of civilians in the western Oromia state.

The Oromo Liberation Army has been inflicting damage on civilians as its fighters fled an offensive by security forces in Oromia, as per reports by Al Jazeera. There were a lot of citizens living in the Qellen Wollega zone of Oromia that have been massacred. Rebels had also managed to attack Gambella, the capital. According to officials, the rebels have been killing the ethnic Amharas. Around three hundred bodies were collected, although there still could be more and their whereabouts are known to no one. Many also believe that places like Tole Kebelle are vulnerable to more rounds of attacks if security forces leave from there.

Michele Bachelet, the United Nations rights chief, has called on the Ethiopian authorities to conduct 'prompt, impartial and thorough' investigations. It is also believed that the Tigray conflict in northern Ethiopia was instigating the persistent cycle of violence against civilians by security forces, which has made the country even more vulnerable.

The al-Shabaab extremist group has exploited Ethiopia's

internal turmoil by crossing the border from neighbouring Somalia and making unprecedented attacks, according to a top US military commander.

Ethiopia, by and large, has long resisted such cross-border attacks by the al-Qaeda-linked al-Shabaab, in part by deploying troops inside Somalia, where the extremist group controls large rural parts of the country's southern and central regions. But, the government of Prime Minister Abiy Ahmed and its security forces have struggled with unrest at home especially since the Tigray conflict began in late 2020, making their foreign deployments less effective.

Matt Bryden, a security analyst with the Sahan Foundation think tank told Associated Press that Al Shabaab's turn to Ethiopia is a significant strategic shift. The planning for their offensives may have begun more than one year ago when the Ethiopian government appeared to be on the verge of collapse. Al-Shabaab has trained several thousand fighters for its Ethiopian 'command,' mainly ethnic Somalis and Oromos inside Ethiopia, according to Bryden. There were also credible reports of al-Shabab units deploying in the direction of Moyale, the main border post between Ethiopia and Kenya. If al-Shabab establishes a stronghold in south-eastern Ethiopia, the consequences for peace and security in the region could be very serious indeed. It is because the fighters would be well-positioned to attack and penetrate deeper into Ethiopia, Kenya and even as far as Uganda to the west. In fact, Al-Shabaab has carried out several high-profile deadly attacks inside Kenya over the years.

The outgoing head of the US Africa Command, Gen. Stephen Townsend, has warned that al-Shabaab activities inside Ethiopia were not a 'one-off' and said the fighters made it as far as one hundred fifty kilometres into the country.

Al-Shabaab has long regarded Ethiopia as an enemy for its long military presence inside Somalia countering the fighters. Via its Radio Andalus media arm, the extremist group has claimed killing at least one hundred eighty-seven Ethiopian regional forces and seized military equipment in its attacks.

As per security analysts Caleb Weiss and Ryan O Farell, Al-Shabaab ultimate aims inside Ethiopia are yet to be determined. Its new actions signal its 'growing ambition, regional capabilities, and opportunism to exploit regional geopolitics.

The Ethiopian government has also blamed Sudan for seizing more land in the Fashaqa triangle by ousting Ethiopian farmers. They also believe that there is a third-party involvement of Egypt in doing so. Egyptians, all along, have remained silent over the Tigray war and occasionally expressed their support for stability at the source of the Nile River. They want to take advantage of Ethiopia's internal turmoil to protect its vital and strategic interests. In moments of frankness, President al-Sisi and Foreign Minister Shukri have stated that Egypt 'will not tolerate' any development upstream that will affect the Nile water flow.

According to an analysis in Adis Standard by Ezekeil Gebissa, professor of history and African studies at the University of Flint, Michigan: 'Because of the meaningless Tigray war, Ethiopia is currently an isolated international pariah whose only friend is Isaias Afeworki of Eritrea, the vilest dictator of the Red Sea basin. It lost its military to war, land to Sudan, the capacity to defend its citizens, and credibility on the international stage. That is a high price to pay to satisfy an ambitious leader's urge for power.'

Due to the recent upscale of the conflict, many survivors in Hawa Gelan Woreda, Lemlem Kebele in Kelem Welega zone of Oromia State are facing various problems due to their displacement from their residencies. The displaced people are currently sheltered in Mechara town where they are receiving support from the local community. Many are also living their life in various camps, where the government has directly given blankets and meagre food items. The displaced people are also unable to attend their farmlands, in the planting season, not only due to security concerns but also due to lack of fertiliser distribution. Most of their cattle is also looted.

According to the latest UN humanitarian report, 'a marked increase of new arrivals (more than 20, 500 people)' is reported across Amhara Region due to 'the current hostilities in Western Oromia.'

'Violence in Western Oromia (the Wollegas) and Southern Oromia (several locations in Guji and West Guji zones) also led to the killing and displacement of civilians, destroying livelihoods and impacting the operations of humanitarian partners. The increased violence in June has reportedly led to large-scale displacement from Gimbi Woreda to Diga Woreda in East Wollega Zone, as well as in Guji and West Guji zones. Insecurity in Oromia is also causing increased displacement into the neighbouring Amhara Region. A marked increase of new arrivals (more than 20,500 people) is reported across Amhara Region due to the current hostilities in western Oromia,' the UN report said.

August 6, 2022

37

TUNISIA'S REFERENDUM LEAVES ITS PEOPLE DIVIDED

Tunisia began its new era of a march towards autocracy when Kais Saied passed a referendum which was met with a low turnout in July 2022. It was something unexpected after he had installed a new female prime minister giving hope to Tunisians for a vibrant democracy.

The new constitution includes changes to shift back power to the presidency, away from parliament, which Saied's supporters see as a centre full of political bickering and government paralysis. His mandated charter would replace a 2014 constitution that was a hard-won compromise between Islamist-leaning and secular forces.

There was no minimum participation rate requirement for the referendum. Hence, the newly drafted constitution will become the law. Tunisian political analyst and author Amine Snoussi made comparisons of this referendum with some other recent referendums in other countries where attendance was far higher, such as Uruguay in 2022, Chile in 2020, or the UK's Brexit vote in 2016.

The most important feature of the new constitution, according to an Op-ed in The New Arab by Alessandra Bajec, is that it would create a 'new council of regions' on par with the assembly of representatives, though it does not provide details on how it would be instituted or what powers it would have. Article 5 of the charter also takes out references to both Islam and the civilian nature of

Tunisia, merely stating that the country 'belongs to the Islamic Ummah' and that the state is required to 'achieve the objectives of Islam in preserving life, honour, money, religion, and freedom', but within a democratic system. According to Bajec, the provision had been previously criticised as it could allow the courts to use this mention of religious principles as a basis for undermining human rights.

Omar Hamady, a constitutional expert also noted the nature of power diversions towards the president. He commented: 'The system now rests on a central institution [the president] around which a multitude of bodies gravitate, and are in one way or another subservient to it, with absolutely no separation of powers that ensures checks and balances.'

Although Saied has assured that he is the new dictator, he says freedoms, the ones mentioned in 2011 are protected. However, the opposition groups have tainted the new development as 'false' and 'not credible', and view it as a dark day in their democracy. According to Nejib Chebbi, head of the opposition National Salvation Front, which includes the Islamist Ennahda party, the biggest faction in the dissolved parliament, Saied 'falsified the political will' by 'falsifying the results.' Aymen Bessalah, a Tunisian non-resident fellow at the Tahrir Institute for Middle East Policy (TIMEP) also believed the development to be dangerous, after ten years of nation-building, and that it runs counter to the idea of a republic.

Add to this, a report by Al Jazeera mentions widespread ideological divisions among anti-Saied forces. The main anti-Saied grouping, Citizens Against the Coup, has faced difficulty attracting support from some on the liberal left because it includes members of the Ennahdha Party amongst its ranks, as well as some other political parties.

There are some local activists, such as Wajdi Mahouchei, who believe that he did not see any changes he wanted in the constitution, and started campaigning online with comedy sketches, satirising him for what he called Saied's strange behaviours. His most popular video is called The President Who Cried Wolf, "because he is always saying 'they want to kill me, but nobody wants to kill him.'"

The new text would place the president in command of the army, will allow him to appoint a government without parliamentary approval, and make it very hard to remove the president from office. He could also present draft laws to parliament, where MPs would be forced to give priority. The new charter gives the president almost all powers and dismantles any check on the ruler, and any institution that might exert any kind of control over the president, as per Said Benarbia, regional director of the International Commission of Jurists.

According to an Op-ed by The New Arab, the Tunisian president had been quite isolated off late, mostly limited his comments to public videos, often against domestic foes, calling them 'snakes,' 'germs' and 'traitors.'

Despite believing that the opposition groups had miserably failed to lead the country to prosperity, Saied's popularity is tempered by soaring inflation and very high youth unemployment, since he won an election in 2019 with a landslide victory. Opinion polls also reflect his dwindling popularity since 2021 or so. Although, a group of small political parties who had stood behind president Saied in 2021, such as the People's Movement (Echaab), Alliance for Tunisia, and Tunisia Forward, have urged people to vote in favour of the draft constitution in the referendum, embodying a resolve to break the deadlock within the past ten years. It is because they do not want Ennahdha to come into power, as they think billions of dinars have been stolen under its eyes. This shows the constitutional amendment is keeping Tunisians divided.

August 15, 2022

38

AMERICAN PLUNDER OF SYRIAN OIL

In July 2022, China Daily reported that US military tankers had carried thousands of litres of crude oil from Syria's north-eastern province of Hasakah into the semi-autonomous Kurdistan region of northern Iraq. The Chinese paper accused Washington of 'bandit behaviour,' claiming that 'stealing oil is their profession.' China's foreign ministry issued a statement urging the United States to respect Syria's sovereignty, lift unilateral sanctions, and 'stop plundering Syria's national resources.'

Syria's official news agency SANA echoed these accusations. In August 2022, it reported that 144 tankers laden with Syrian oil crossed into Iraq via the al-Mahmoudiya border, only days after another convoy of 60 vehicles passed through the al-Waleed crossing. SANA described these transfers as violations of international law, portraying US forces as occupiers.

The Pentagon, however, has consistently maintained that its deployment in north-eastern Syria is aimed at preventing oilfields from falling into the hands of ISIS extremists. US troops have been stationed in Deir Ezzor and Hasakah since 2015, working alongside the Syrian Democratic Forces (SDF). Damascus rejects this explanation, insisting that Washington's true purpose is to exploit Syria's mineral wealth. Former President Donald Trump reinforced this perception when he openly stated in 2019 that US forces were in Syria 'for the oil', contradicting his own officials during a meeting with Turkey's President Erdogan.

According to Syria's Ministry of Oil and Mineral Resources, Washington is stealing more than 80 per cent of the country's daily oil output. Official figures claimed that in the first half of 2022 Syria produced 14.5 million barrels, averaging 80,300 barrels per day. Of this, 66,000 barrels - about 83 per cent - were allegedly taken by US forces. These claims, reported by SANA and repeated by Russian and Chinese media, were said to be backed by footage and photographs. Independent verification, however, remains limited.

The accusations extend beyond oil. As Steve Sweeney wrote in Morning Star Online, US forces have also been accused of smuggling wheat and even gold, leaving Syrians hungry under the weight of sanctions. He argued that the Caesar Syria Civilian Protection Act, signed by Trump in 2020, has blocked aid to Syria until Bashar al-Assad leaves power, worsening economic chaos. Sweeney suggested that journalists are often too afraid to report openly on alleged US resource theft, and claimed that even the SDF has confirmed such practices.

The SDF itself has been accused of handing over oil reserves to local companies to prevent them falling back under Assad's control. This reflects the complex politics of north-east Syria, where Kurdish forces balance between American support and local autonomy. The controversial oil deal between the SDF and US firm Delta Crescent Energy, struck in 2020, expired in April 2021 after President Joe Biden cancelled a waiver that had allowed trading in Syria.

The human cost of these disputes is evident. Syrian journalist Mohammad al-Saghir has reportedly been detained since 2019 by armed groups in north-east Syria, allegedly for reporting on oil and wheat theft. His case highlights the dangers faced by local reporters in a region where multiple militias and foreign forces operate.

Russia has also seized on the allegations. In July 2022, President Vladimir Putin accused the United States of 'looting' Syrian oil while simultaneously imposing sanctions on Damascus. He demanded that US forces withdraw from the east Euphrates, warning that their presence had produced 'disastrous results.'

The scale of US control is significant. American forces occupy more than 30 per cent of Syrian territory, including oil-rich regions such as Deir Ezzor, Hasakah, and Raqqa. These areas have long attracted interest from US energy corporations, some of which had ties to the Trump administration.

The broader context is one of geopolitical rivalry. China and Russia amplify allegations of US oil theft to undermine Washington's legitimacy in Syria. Syrian state media portrays the US as an occupying power, while American officials insist their mission is counter-terrorism. Independent observers note that while US forces do oversee oilfields, the revenues are often channelled through the SDF to fund local administration rather than being shipped to America. Yet the secrecy surrounding these operations fuels suspicion.

The accusations of wheat theft add another layer. Syria, once self-sufficient in grain, has faced shortages since the war began. Sanctions and conflict have disrupted supply chains, leaving millions food insecure.

Reports of US convoys carrying grain into Iraq, whether

accurate or not, resonate strongly with Syrians enduring hunger.

Narratively, the story of Syria's oil encapsulates the tragedy of the war. A country devastated by conflict, sanctions, and foreign intervention sees its resources contested by external powers.

For Damascus, the oilfields symbolise sovereignty lost. For Washington, they represent leverage against ISIS and Assad. For Moscow and Beijing, they are evidence of American hypocrisy.

Ultimately, the allegations of US oil theft in Syria remain politically charged. While China and Syria have repeatedly accused the US of 'banditry,' independent verification is scarce.

What is clear is that Syria's oilfields have become a focal point of international rivalry, with civilians suffering from shortages and economic collapse.

August 16, 2022

39

FACTIONALISM INSIDE BRITISH LABOUR PARTY

Forde Inquiry Report has exposed factionalism within the British Labour Party, during Jeremy Corbyn's tenure. This was made public in July 2022, after an earlier leaked internal report. The new report was originally intended to be published by the end of 2020 but it faced difficulties because of continuing legal battles within the party, and its publication was repeatedly delayed.

The report confirms a disturbing picture as the party's democratic socialism was pitted against rightist bureaucracy. The party even committed to maintaining the neoliberal priorities of New Labour set by former leader Tony Blair.

Many of the party staff saw one of their main aims in finding reasons to expel Corbyn supporters, in what they termed as 'trot busting' and 'trot hunting' exercises. It is believed that some party staff members exhibited 'deplorably factional and insensitive, and at times discriminatory attitudes' towards Corbyn's supporters.

Since Corbyn's departure, there has been a mass exodus of members disillusioned with the direction the party has been taking. Forde, who was commissioned by Corbyn's successor, Keir Starmer, to investigate turbulent years, proposed ways to deal with divisions that have threatened to tear Labour apart.

Starmer had criticised what he calls a 'monoculture' and 'groupthink' at the head office, which had ultimately damaged British Labour Party's overall effectiveness.

The report even alleges a continuation of factionalism by other means, which includes Corbyn's wielding of factional power which was more than the combined might of Labour headquarters, the parliamentary party, and the entire media establishment. It had eventually fed paranoia to its opponents within the party.

The Blairists, by contrast, listened empathetically to any story by journalists that could be spun against Corbyn. The report had indicted Corbyn as 'shambolic,' 'feeble minded,' 'traitor' and a 'national security threat.'

The enquiry even affirms that Labour staff secretly allocated 'money to fund' campaigns supportive of largely anti-Corbyn MPs, while withholding funds from 'campaigns for pro-Corbyn candidates in potentially Tory winnable seats.'

Starmer, in fact, had failed to find a middle ground, between Labour's left and right, and stoked fires from one side only. The 'broad church projects,' which Forde espouses as a way forward, were discarded by Starmer at every turn.

Not only Starmer was responsible to force Corbyn out of the party, but he also exiled some of his supporters to backbenches, and drove the whole party to the Blairite territory. Many leftists within the party are made miserable in the new environment in such a way that the only choice for them is to leave, showing that they want to eradicate every chance of left-wing membership, and having an influence over the party policy again.

There are also reports where WhatsApp chains reveal internal sabotage from the Labour rightists such as 'deliberate go slow by certain members of staff designed to frustrate the efforts of a colleague from Corbyn's section to promote party's wider interests.'

The leaked report also made grave allegations of misogyny and racism exhibited by senior party staff. It made a tough reading because of the ugly picture painted by the report. Forde had claimed that messages in the leaked report were 'not cherry picked and selectively edited,' and they betrayed 'overt and underlying racism and sexism' and 'deplorable, factional, insensitive,' and at times 'discriminatory attitudes.'

According to a Guardian Op-ed by Elliot Chappell, Forde had found that the leftist section of Labour was operating a hierarchy of racism, because of the attention given to anti-Semitism, and its relationship to inter-factional conflict, with other forms of discrimination ignored. As per the Op-ed, WhatsApp messages, in reference to left-wing MP Diane Abbott, Forde described them as expressions of 'visceral disgust, drawing on racist tropes.'

In fact, Starmer has demonstrated the true meaning of factionalism within the party. According to Jonathan Cook's Op-ed in Middle East Eye: 'The right will permanently treat the left as unwanted interlopers, and refuse any ideological compromise.' But, Starmer's supporters have been giving absurd claims that he has rid the party of destructive factionalism, and of an unacceptable culture which led to its defeat in elections in 2019.

When it came to winning the recent elections, 'both factions were trying to win in different ways.' But both sides did not have equal mandate to fight and win the election. That is why, according to Chappell, what the Labour right did was not fight the election 'in a different way', as Forde suggests. They rather staged an internal coup that made the Labour Party internally dysfunctional and made it increasingly ill-equipped to form a government.

In the 2019 election, Labour was in open disarray due to this very reason. This also gave Starmer the chance to step in for unity, who promised to restore calm and find common ground between left and right. But the reality is that Starmer deceived the leadership, as he became more than a battering ram for Labour right. It is also making Forde hesitant to conclude that factionalism after the enquiry is far worse, and that party's internal democracy is having a more distant prospect than ever.

August 18, 2022

40

SIERRA LEONE ROCKED BY PROTESTS

In August 2022, Freetown in Sierra Leone exploded into violence due to persistent economic hardships, and a government failure in ameliorating the impact of rising costs. As clashes broke out, most of the dwellers of Freetown stayed indoors.

People believed it was a sudden explosion of violence, as many government buildings and private property were destroyed. Due to this, government forces patrolled the streets, and a tense, eerie calm returned with ordinary life gradually returning.

But, due to the intensity of the protests common people were shocked. Apart from Freetown, the protests had been also concentrated in the opposition's northern heartland. Female protestors had too joined the political protestors, and it added to the mayhem.

It was unclear who was behind the destruction, but Freetown's mayor, Yvonne Aki Sawyerr, an opponent to the current government, revealed in a statement in August 2022 that the city council was not responsible for it. Abdul Rashid Thomas, wrote in an Oped for Sierra Leone Telegraph that the destruction of property by protestors was uncalled for, despite the constitution guaranteeing the right to protest and peaceful demonstrations.

It also seems that the youth in Sierra Leone, largely unemployed, who drove the crises, have repeatedly been misused, abused, and refused on several fronts. The civil war in the past has been fresh in their minds, and it gave them a stimulus for violence, including beating police officers to death.

It was during President Kabba's time when he had promised that the Truth and Reconciliation was a process that needed to be put in order, to ensure peace was safeguarded. However, this promise for peaceful reforms was strained during Koroma's presidency, eventually resulting in a transition from the All-People's Conference to Sierra Leone Peoples Party in the 2018 elections. It was hoped under President Bio that the arrangement of peace would be strengthened and his government would usher the change. Until now, most people are not satisfied, it seems. In fact, people have witnessed the use of extra-judicial measures, such as disappearances, intimidation and killings which were commonplace under the NPRC / AFRC era with the specific aim of silencing the collective voice.

The role of the church in pacifying the crises during the protests was also highlighted in the media. As the president, and some of the cabinet members are catholic, the catholic church had issued statements, to put out Christian values in place to promote the common good, and a good life for everybody.

According to World Bank data, more than half of the population live below the poverty line, so the venting out of people's frustration was meant to happen eventually.

Due to the war in Ukraine, the country was badly affected by inflation, like many other African countries. It was also affected by Ebola and coronavirus outbreaks.

Sierra Leone had enjoyed relative stability since it emerged from a civil war between 1991 and 2002 that, according to the United Nations, left at least 70,000 people dead and 2.6 million displaced. But it remains among the world's poorest countries despite its extensive mineral resources. Nearly thirty per cent of Sierra Leone's population suffers from chronic hunger, according to the World Food Program. For agriculturalists, the situation is also troublesome as the cost of fertilisers has spiked.

According to an Op-ed in New York Times, by Elian Peltier and Yaya Barry, Sierra Leone's central bank removed three zeros from its banknotes in July 2022, hoping to restore confidence in the currency and reduce the amount of paper money in circulation while keeping its value unchanged.

In a leaked report by Politico, Sierra Leone is also struggling with food imports. Food accounts for about a third of merchandise imports in Sierra Leone.

The government had accused the opposition of inciting the demonstrations. The country's vice president, Mohammed Juldeh Jalloh in a televised speech in August 2022 had said that 'for the last several weeks some self-serving Sierra Leoneans have intensified the call for violence and the forceful overthrow of the legitimate government of President Julius Maada Bio.' The president himself in another media interview described this week's protests as acts of terrorism. It has been believed that a Sierra Leonean citizen residing in Holland has been accused of instigating the insurrection.

According to police spokesman Brima Kamara, the ex-pat was believed to be using various accounts on Facebook to spread hate against the ruling SLPP party. That is why to curb the situation, the Internet had been blocked at several places, to stop the protests from spreading. It also led to the arrest of more than a hundred persons.

As an answer to this, the United Nations, the European Union, and the United States issued pleas for calm in August 2022. Amnesty International also urged the Sierra Leonean authorities to hold accountable those responsible for the deaths of protesters.

August 22, 2022

41

POLITICS BEHIND NARCO TRADE AT JORDAN'S BORDER

Jordan has recently intensified its warnings against Iranian militias along its northern frontier, accusing Tehran of facilitating drug trafficking through drones and other methods. Officials in Amman argue that Iranian-affiliated groups have expanded their influence in southern Syria, shifting the balance of power in the area. Al Jazeera reported that Jordanian authorities see narcotics smuggling as not only a criminal enterprise but also a geopolitical weapon, with militias using the trade to fund operations.

These warnings are not new. Since Tehran intervened in the Syrian war in 2014 to support President Bashar al-Assad, Jordan has been wary of being drawn into the conflict. By late 2021, drug smuggling had escalated and become increasingly violent. In January 2022, a Jordanian army officer was killed and three personnel injured when smugglers opened fire on an outpost along the border, according to Reuters.

The situation prompted Jordan's military leadership to adopt harsher tactics. In January 2021, the chairman of the Joint Chiefs of Staff ordered a change in the rules of engagement, introducing what The Jordan Times described as a 'shoot to kill policy' against smugglers. Shortly afterwards, the army announced that it had killed twenty-seven smugglers and seized 17,348 sheets of hashish and more than sixteen million narcotic pills.

BasNews later confirmed that Jordanian forces continued to apply this policy, killing four smugglers in June 2025.

Jordanian officials said they had contacted Syrian counterparts for explanations but received no response. At one-point, Jordanian forces reported that dead smugglers were found wearing Syrian army uniforms. Analysts writing in The Washington Post suggested that members of Assad's 4th Armoured Division, commanded by his brother Maher, were implicated in the trade. The Media Line added in 2025 that remnants of the division were linked to organised crime rings, even as Syrian authorities occasionally intercepted smuggling attempts themselves.

The Jordan–Syria border stretches 375 kilometres across rugged terrain from the Golan Heights to the Iraqi frontier, making it difficult to police. In one eastern pocket outside government control, the commander of the US-backed opposition group Jaysh Maghawir al-Thawra told Middle East Eye that his area, which includes the Rukhban camp, is surrounded by Iranian militias aiming to depopulate it. He argued that Jordan is seen by these groups as the main transit point to the Gulf for Captagon, a cheap amphetamine produced in Syria.

The Centre for Operational Analysis and Research estimated that Captagon exports from Syria reached a market value of at least $3.46 billion in 2020. The Financial Times described Jordan as a 'transit country for smugglers,' with most narcotics passing through to Saudi Arabia, where demand is high. FDD's Long War Journal reported in June 2024 that Jordanian authorities seized 9.5 million Captagon pills in one operation, implicating Hezbollah, and Iran-backed militias as masterminds. Hezbollah has denied involvement, but The Guardian and The New York Times have linked the group to narcotics operations in Syria and Lebanon.

Beyond security concerns, stability in southern Syria is vital for Jordan's economy, which has struggled for years. World Bank data shows sluggish GDP growth since 2009, while The New Arab highlighted in 2022 that Jordan hosts more than 1.2 million Syrians, costing its treasury over one billion dollars annually. Mamdouh al-Abadi, former deputy prime minister, told Al-Arabiya that good neighbourly agreements have kept Jordan safe, noting that no Iranian bombing has occurred on Jordanian soil. Since 2018, Amman has sought to upgrade diplomatic ties with Damascus, hoping to reopen the Nasib-Jaber crossing, a key trade route. The crossing was partially reopened in 2018 but closed again in 2021 due to renewed clashes.

Historically, southern Syria has been closely linked to northern Jordan, both once part of the Ottoman province of Hauran. British and French imperial borders divided families and tribes, but ties remained strong. Early in the Syrian war, Hauranis crossed into Jordan to shelter with relatives. These connections fostered trade links, with southern Syria and northern Jordan economically dependent on each other. Syria provides Jordan with access to the Mediterranean and overland routes to Europe, while Jordan offers Syria access to the Red Sea and Gulf markets.

Despite cultural and economic closeness, political differences have long caused tensions. Christopher Philips wrote in Middle East Eye that since 1963 Syria has been ruled by Baathist autocrats hostile to the West, in contrast to Jordan's pro-Western Hashemite monarchy. During the Cold War, they backed opposing blocs. In 1970, Syria briefly invaded Jordan in support of Palestinian guerrillas fighting the Hashemites. A decade later, Jordan supported

Muslim Brotherhood militants against the Syrian regime. Yet there were also phases of cooperation: both fought Israel in 1967 and 1973. Relations soured in the 1980s when they supported opposite sides in the Iran-Iraq War, but warmed in the 1990s during the Arab-Israeli peace process.

Ties deteriorated again in the mid-2000s when Jordan aligned with US efforts to isolate Syria after the 2005 assassination of Lebanese Prime Minister Rafiq Hariri, but improved when that isolation failed. Analysts in The Guardian note that Jordan's pragmatic diplomacy often shifts with regional currents. The current round of friendship, marked by attempts to reopen trade routes, may collapse into enmity if another crisis pits Amman and Damascus against each other. Yet history suggests such hostilities eventually subside, reflecting the cyclical nature of Jordan–Syria relations.

Jordan's accusations against Iranian militias highlight the intersection of security, economics, and geopolitics. The drug trade has become a multi-billion-dollar industry funding militias and destabilising borders. Amman's adoption of harsher military tactics reflects the seriousness of the threat. At the same time, Jordan's economy depends on cross-border stability, making cooperation with Damascus essential. The challenge for Jordan is balancing its security concerns with its economic needs, while navigating the influence of Iran, Hezbollah, and the Syrian regime. As Reuters concluded, Jordan's frontier has become a testing ground for regional rivalries, where narcotics, militias and geopolitics converge.

August 29, 2022

42

CHAOS IN IRAQ AFTER SADR CALLED IT QUITS

In late August 2022, Muqtada al Sadr went on Twitter to announce his resignation from politics.

Sometime before, when Grand Ayatollah Kadhim al Haeri, whose followers contain many Sadrists, had resigned as well, he had asked the Shia population to obey Iran's leader, Ayatollah Ali Khameini. For some watchers, this was seen as an attempt to weaken the Sadrist movement in Iraq.

After Sadr's tweet, thousands of his followers stormed the Iraqi capital Green Zone, the Republican palace, and key government buildings in Baghdad. Since then, the Iraqi capital has witnessed strong intra Shia-confrontations, between Sadr's supporters and variety of armed groups loyal to different factions, within the Shia Coordination Framework, a pro-Iran set of parties. Hundreds have been injured and tens killed. To save his reputation, Sadr apologised to the Iraqi people for the bloodshed.

As per an Op-ed by Hussein Ibish, Sadr's political career did not start with an extraordinary example. He wrote: 'Sadr's career has been built on the legacy of his father and uncle, two of the most revered Shiite religious authorities of their generation. While he lacks their erudition and religious credentials, and had no governmental experience, Sadr succeeded in building religious and political authority in tandem, each complementing the other. And that has made him a remarkably toxic figure in contemporary Iraq.'

Since prevailing in October 2021 elections, Sadr has been failing to convert his political hindsight into practical political power. He is not entirely at fault, as his pro-Iranian Shiite rivals are more reckless, dangerous, and violent, while Kurdish groups are hopelessly divided, and Sunni factions are split largely between groups aligned with different Gulf Arab patrons.

As a reaction, neighbouring Iran announced it was closing all land borders with Iraq until further notice and warned citizens not to travel to Iraq, as the country was working to return Iranian visitors home safely. Tehran's international airport suspended flights to Baghdad. Millions of Iranian pilgrims travel to Iraq every year to visit historic shrines at the heart of Shiite Muslim identity.

Al-Kadhimi, the prime minister suspended cabinet sessions until further notice. In an appeal to Sadr, he said perpetuating political disputes 'to the point of damaging all state institutions does not serve the Iraqi people, their aspirations, their future and their territorial integrity.' He even expressed regret that the political conflict had reached the level of the use of weapons among Iraqi factions.

Going back to Iraq's October 2021 parliamentary elections, Sadr emerged with the single largest number of seats. He allied with other two major winners of the election: the Sunni Sovereignty Alliance and the Kurdistan Democratic Party. At that time, Sadr's attempt at government formation faced strong resistance, mainly from the Coordination Framework. As per an Op-ed by Kamaran Palani on Al Jazeera: 'This bloc has been calling for the continuation of the classical post-2003 consensus model of governance, under which an administration effectively needs to enjoy a two-thirds majority, and not just a simple one, to rule. While this grouping did not win anywhere close to the numbers itself, it had enough seats in parliament to block the Sadrists from claiming the support of two-thirds of the legislature.'

Then, in February 2022, the Iraqi supreme court, being carried away by Iranian influence, interpreted the Iraqi constitution in a way that turned the need for a two-thirds majority into an edict. Effectively, this means that any Iraqi government must be an administration of consensus, a failed approach that escalated violence in Iraq. However, Sadr is adamant on a post 2003 system.

As Sadr failed to form the government, he shocked everyone by ordering seventy-three of his lawmakers to resign from parliament in June 2022. That was a huge mistake. According to Palani, his political strength against his rivals within the Shia community comes from two main cards: his seats in parliament and the loyalty of his strong and disciplined base. Although, his clerical and rabble-rousing qualities did not let him have a firm understanding of the economic and patronage gamesmanship involved in government formation in a parliamentary system.

That is why the elections themselves will not solve Iraq's political dysfunction, as there is no common ground between Sadrists and Coordination Framework. After Sadr's resignation, he no doubt will have no say in the parliament but his hold over common people on streets means that he can bring down any government in Baghdad. Some analysts also believe that his resignation is temporary, and that he may brace himself for next elections.

September 28, 2022

43

RADICAL ITALY OF MELONI

Giorgia Meloni is the first female prime minister Italy ever had, after swearing office with a coalition in October 2022. Unapologetically intense, she is also known as a political charmer in known circles. As a youth activist in the post-Fascist Italian Social Movement, she and her militant coterie had nicknames like Frodo and Hobbit, and they revered Lord of the Rings, and other works by British writer, J.R.R Tolkien. They also visited schools in character and huddled at the sounding of the horn of Boromir for cultural chats. She attended 'Hobbit Camp' and sang along with the extremist folk band Compagnia dell'Anello, or Fellowship of the Ring.

At 19, she told a French Television that Mussolini was a great leader, and that he did everything right for the country. But, after being part of the national alliance in 2006, she changed her perception and believed that 'dictators' do make mistakes, and that Mussolini was no good when he talked about racial laws, authoritarianism, and entering World War II on the side of Adolf Hitler. She also refused to change her party logo, which is also used by the Italian Social Movement, believing that the 'flame' in it has nothing to do with fascism.

In her career, Meloni was also the youngest minister to hold office in Italy at 31, and co-founded Brothers of Italy in 2012. Her election win is often credited for being in the opposition. She also started to reassure those who questioned her lack of experience with her slogan 'Ready'.

Wary of Italy's huge debt, she has been vehement about fiscal prudence, despite her coalition's call for tax cuts, and higher social spending. In her fight against the current EU bureaucracy, she is toeing the line with Hungarian Prime Minister Victor Orban, who is also accused of fascist leanings, although now she no longer confronts the idea of EU's single currency.

On several occasions in her campaigns, Meloni has tried to distance herself from her fascist past though, which will make mainstream Italian politics more sceptical. Despite expounding the idea of Catholic values, she in her election speeches wanted to govern for all Italians. This makes her political orientation complex, or hypocritical at worse.

Nevertheless, it has been a long journey for Meloni, from being a teen activist to the prime minister. Often provocative in her speeches, due to her gender ideology, 'Italy First' campaigns, and the need for Italians to raise more children, she also rallies against many prevailing ideas of EU, mass immigration, and LGBT lobbies. Her main target has been what she calls 'the left', by which she really means the centre-left Democratic Party. In fact, to confront migration, she wants a naval blockade of Libyan boats leaving their shores. She often derogatorily refers to migrants as *clandestini* ('illegals'). According to her shallow perceptions, all undocumented migrants in Italy end up as drug dealers or sex workers.

Meloni is also labelled as the 'European Trump' by some sections of the press, due to positions which have been described as fruits of racism, bigotry, and white supremacy, but as she has praised Iran and Hezbollah, this stance may not be clearer to perceive. It is maybe due to this reason, some American politicians are not totally bewitched by Meloni, and demand that her politics deserves careful watching.

In a 2019 speech, she won many common American fans. It includes women because white feminism has become an integral component of crypto-fascistic and white nationalist cabals in the United States. Among Meloni's admirers are also male commentators like Rod Dreher and Texas Sen. Ted Cruz also called her speech video 'spectacular'. Dreher, however, also believes that Meloni's reporting in America should not be largely believed as it is been done by the liberal press in bondage with their progressive ideology. Although, a Washington Post Op-ed criticised her speech, flaking it as 'not making sense.' But, according to an article by Jennifer Graham in Desert News, it did nevertheless make sense to a wide audience of Americans, 'who were weary of being dismissed as neanderthals and bigots for believing something is not quite right with her country's rush to embrace gender-affirming surgery and to throw out perfectly good pronouns.'

Graham's intellectual posture may be right on this, because Meloni has in fact weaponised sexual assault on non-Italian women in her campaigns, by posting a video of a Ukrainian woman, living in Italy, being raped by a Guinean asylum seeker. She tried to make it viral, to re-traumatise women, as the video was widely circulated on social media. That is why Natasha Noman, an MSNBC columnist, wrote: 'Meloni is as much a feminist as a wolf in sheep's clothing is a sheep. In co-opting an identity and cause that she then weaponises to attack the very same people the cause is intended to protect, figures like Meloni present a much greater threat to feminism than cisgender men.'

When it comes to some of her other economic policies,

Meloni wants to revisit Italian reforms agreed upon with the EU in return for almost €200bn (£178bn) in post-Covid recovery grants and loans, arguing that the energy crisis has changed the situation. As per BBC, Italy is already the second most indebted country in the eurozone, and Prof Leila Simona Talani of King's College London believes the next government will face a clutch of serious issues. Although, Prof Gianluca Passarrelli of Rome's Sapienza University told the BBC that Meloni will be stern in her economic policies, and will give a reason to cheer for her followers.

That is why, it is not surprising that the flowing dialogue with the outgoing prime minister, who was also a former president of the European Central Bank, to the point where we have already seen insinuations that Draghi has become Meloni's mentor and guarantor, reflects of some optimism.

Meloni's win as prime minister is also another reason to believe that the culture wars of populist propaganda that brought the post-ideological Five Star Movement and the far-right League into power in 2018 was reflective of an already deteriorating environment. Add to that, Meloni's win is a defeat to most vulnerable communities and for progressive activists and politicians who are unwilling to compromise on their values for electoral gain, ushering an era of illiberalism.

October 23, 2022

44

CHILE REJECTS CONSTITUTIONAL CHANGE

To find a solution for discontent among the masses, Chile embarked on a risky and courageous path, to rewrite the constitution to face myriad challenges. Quite lately, they did in October 2020, but it sadly has been rejected by the masses. It is mainly because maximum of the Chilean voters identifies themselves as centrist. Its failure was something extraordinary, as rarely in the modern world has the public rebuffed a constitution-replacement project. It was also a pointer to watchers that Chile, at this moment in time, rejects a plurinational state, as autonomy would have been provided to its indigenous groups.

If the constitution would have been drafted, it would have resulted in one of the most progressive constitutions in the world. According to a Foreign Policy Op-ed by Catherine Osborne, it would have paved the way for stronger protections for indigenous Chileans, empowered labour unions, given environment-friendly laws, and almost would have legalised abortion. It would have also upped the ante for the state's necessities to provide social goods such as health care and housing.

As per an article in The Conversation by Christine Bell, the constitutional change was also including an element of direct democracy, gender parity, and a restructuring of the bicameral parliamentary system to give the chamber of deputies (the lower house) more power at the expense of the senate. It would have inserted more than a hundred rights in Chile's national charter and would have certainly provided a 'cradle to grave' welfare system. Some laws also sounded odd such as 'culturally appropriate food' and 'digital disconnection to the ruinous.'

As vast majority of centrist voters have been recognised, the new process of constitutional reform may be guided by a centrist set of authors, as Boric's government believes that the architects of the constitutional change went wrong. Writing for Nueva Sociedad, Titelman reflected that independent and left-wing figures did not care to have a consensus or compromise regarding the matter with more conservative members. Instead, they had opted for maximalist positions. Assembly member Patricio Fernandez, a journalist who ran for the assembly as an independent candidate, made a similar comment to El Mostrador en La Clave Radio. Rosa Catrileo, an indigenous Mapuche assembly member, also cited poor communication as an impediment to the proposed constitution's approval.

As per an LSE blog, the new set of voters was also the reason for rejection. However, it did not stop a section of Chileans to storm the streets of Santiago to celebrate the constitution's rejection. According to BBC, President Boric insisted that he would now work to achieve a 'text that will incorporate the lessons of the process and win over a broad majority of citizens.' But what is ironic is that Chileans have rejected an attempt to cleanse social and political injustice from their society.

The voters were also disgruntled by the draft's 'vagueness', 'lengthy nature' and the 'legal insecurity', as per an article by Oliver Stuenkel in Carnegie Endowment. Although, the process created an uncanny environment for the prospective investors, as they were unsure about the prospects of the constitutional referendum. The environment-friendly laws would have certainly put the brakes on the production of Chile's copper and lithium mining industries.

Before the referendum, political polarisation deepened, since the protests that happened in 2019. During the weeks prior to the plebiscite, fake news flooded social media in Chile, which included false information that the new constitution would allow abortions 'up to the ninth month of pregnancy' and would abolish private property. Similar tactics may affect public opinion about the next drafting process, too. According to Marta Lagos of Latinobarometro, a polling organisation, August 2022 was 'the dirtiest and most violent month of electoral campaigning that Chile has had since 1989.'

Boric, whose coalition includes both centrists and members of the Communist Party, will have to ensure that the topic does not lead to government infighting and more social chaos. The rejection, in fact, is a devastating blow for progressive politics in Chile, which cannot let go off Pinochet's legacy of a neoliberal constitution.

The weakening of copper prices in Chile is reflective of a recession that would plunge Chile into great griefs. Just six months into his administration, Boric would need sidekicks from elected politicians who did not approve of his policies, a tough thing to ask for, in a time where he has failed to curb inflation and rising crime as well.

After the rejection of changes, it is not yet clear how to move forward. In fact, a new constitution can also be directly called. It seems that the rules for the election of the constitutional convention would not be the same as in the previous process, with its structure, number of participants and work period likely set to change.

October 26, 2022

45

IRANIANS RAGING ON THE STREETS AGAIN

After the death in custody of Mahsa Amini, a young Kurd, who died in a coma, with skull injuries on a ventilator, for 'inappropriate dress' by the moral police, the intellectual assertions of George Orwell become fitting for Iran's new protest movement. He believed that revolutions did not come by chance, but by reason and that revolutionaries of the past become new tyrants, only to be toppled again. Iran's foundations as a theocracy seem wobbling because this is not the first time in recent memory that Iranians are at odds with their leaders.

In 2009, millions of adults took to the street over alleged fraud in the presidential election. It was called the Green Movement, which was largely urban and middle class. At that time, they rallied around two losing candidates, waved massive banners demanding democracy, and women wore headscarves, sashes, and paint in a vivid shade of green. As a counter-reaction, hundreds were convicted in Stalinesque mass trials back then. Protests erupted again over the price of eggs and poultry, in 2017, and over price hikes for gas, in 2018. Then, 2019 was also a massive year for dissent which was snubbed violently. The demonstrations in 2022 are rawer, centred largely on school and university campuses with street bonfires where girls and women are cutting their hair and taking off and burning their hijabs. The movement is, so far, largely leaderless. Press with its photographs and videos have broadcasted soul-crushing scenes, as protesters know only what they are against. 'Death to the dictator' and 'Mullahs get lost' have been popular slurs targeting the Supreme Leader, Ayatollah Ali Khamenei.

Men and boys have joined in as well, reflecting that they too are unhappy with the system, and need an alternative. According to Daniel Edelstein, a political scientist, one of the few possible parallels to this revolution was the role of Parisian female *poissonieres*, or market workers, who stormed Versailles to prevent the king from turning against the National Assembly and crushing the nascent French Revolution. However, what makes this revolution unique is that the upheaval is about women's freedom, and that is what makes it special as well. This event is also something like bread riots led by women in Petrograd during the tsarist empire collapse.

The state murder of Amini has unusually gotten more press attention than previous cases which refused to make headlines.

What is worrying for the Iranian grey-bearded theocrats is that people, including children who have died, will provide a stimulus for more protests, as in Shiite Islam, deaths are commemorated again after forty days, which will also provide newer confrontations with the police, giving rise to more causalities. The likelihood of new funerals will provide a similar background that generated the rhythm of Iran's Revolution in 1978 that prompted the Shah to flee in 1979. Hence, the protestors are intensifying domestic woes, at a time when US sanctions have tanked Tehran's currency and limited its oil exports.

According to Robin Wright's New Yorker Op-ed, 'Iran's revolutionaries planted the seeds of their own unravelling.' It is because the feminist movement in Iran is strong as they make up most of the university system, yet they are underrepresented in the labour force. The protests are also happening at a looming transition which might happen in the guardian council leadership soon, as the current supreme leader is ill and battling prostate issues.

Pondering on the leadership crises in the guardian council, to calm down the flaring moods, it likely led Ebrahim Raisi to render a public apology to the people, where he admitted to certain 'weaknesses' and 'shortcomings' in the political system. It might sound cynical at the same time because he has employed counter-demonstrators in universities wearing black chadors, and clamped down Internet access as well.

The protest seems reminiscent of an old idea: let the will of common Iranians be reflected in the political system. But outsiders cannot help much, as Iran has fewer friends around.

As hardliners try to have a grip on every aspect of social life, the feminist movement has grown even more strong. It can be ascertained with an example of International Women's Day in March 2019, when several women activists in Tehran took their hijab off on the subway and handed out flowers to each other.

Commoners also believe it that Raisi has tried to instigate more fear among women. In 2022, he ordered a new Hijab and Chastity law, in which women who posted pictures without the hijab online would be deprived of some social rights for six months to one year. The reason for it is that hijab-wearing women represent the continuation of the Islamic republic. Once that is gone, it will be hard for the clergy junta to improvise power in future.

October 28, 2022

46

RISHI SUNAK LEADS A TUMULTUOUS UNITED KINGDOM

Rishi Sunak became prime minister of the United Kingdom in October 2022 amid a serious political disorder. He has been UK's third prime minister in less than seven weeks' time. But nevertheless, as he is the first prime minister of colour in the United Kingdom, several political analysts thought that his win as prime minister is their Barack Obama moment. It made former cabinet minister, Sajid Javid remark: 'Britain is the most successful multiracial democracy on Earth and proud of this historic achievement.' Although Pankaj Mishra in an adverse criticism in his Guardian Op-ed called him just an upper caste Hindu who is against alcohol and beef eating, and that now snotty-nosed racists like him will try to present themselves as 'purveyors of racial diversity.'

Sunak's fate took a turn when he tried to replace Boris Johnson but he came narrowly behind Liz Truss in the summer of 2022. As Truss staged two embarrassing budget U-turns, scrapping tax cuts for the richest earners and on company profits, it sent shockwaves into the UK economy. It forced her to resign only after forty-four days in office, the shortest time for any British prime minister in history.

Her resignation gave Sunak another reason to taste power as prime minister. Luck also favoured him as Boris Johnson stopped his campaign for a second tenure. With this, he became the youngest prime minister in British history in this century at the age of 42.

An Oxford-educated son of immigrant parents, he first worked at Goldman Sachs and as a former hedge fund partner. After marrying the daughter of Infosys co-founder Murthy, he was valued at 730 million pounds, becoming the richest member of the British parliament, making him even richer than King Charles.

Although, the critics in their assertions have not shied away to conclude that his appointment is a 'vampire-like return of Boris Johnson from the political grave.' They think that Sunak will be a continuer of Truss's policies which were about massive government borrowing from global financial oligarchs, including tax rises and more austerity. In fact, some of his own circles in the Conservative party call him 'illegitimate' with no mandate of any kind. 'Some even think Sunak has organised some sort of globalist Remainer conspiracy, encompassing the civil service, the "mainstream media," the Bank of England, the IMF, the City, Wall Street and the trading rooms of east Asia,' wrote Sean O'Grady in Independent.

It is an unholy pattern. His predecessor, Truss comically paraded effective economic plans, titled 'mini-budget,' and promised 'biggest plans in generations,' sending a clear signal that her government was interested in the economic prosperity of the British people, only to ditch them later.

There are also distinct affirmations coming from the UK press that Sunak does not reflect the common lives of immigrants, south Asians in particular. It is because he is not from London, Manchester, Birmingham, Liverpool, Leeds, Bristol, Sheffield, or towns like Luton, Blackburn, or Wolverhampton, to which Asians came to work since the last century. He is from Southampton, which is far more homogeneous, for an ethnic minority life. So, in that sense, he cannot truly reflect the immigrant lives that most of them have endured.

Sunak also has tough days ahead, as millions of workers are pushing for strike action, as increased poverty engulfs them. Just like Labour, factional divisions are also tearing Tories apart, which he must eventually pacify. It is also cynical that a party which has introduced the most racist campaign in British history, including 'Little England,' a noisome manifestation of British nationalism that led to Brexit, to restore its colonial glories, talks of multiracial pluralism. In fact, the Conservatives are also a party that drafted a debatable report where it is concluded that institutional racism does not exist in British society. Is now Sunak's appointment a face-saving exercise for the world? It does not seem so because he has wholeheartedly supported those policies and other right-wing rants.

Sunak remains deeply out of touch with reality, in a country, he will soon run. Only an assuring accent will not calm the financial markets. He seems to be a devotee to small-state Thatcherism, with no visible concern for the poorest. In March 2020, he promised to bring family benefits in line with inflation. Will he deliver on it now, or was it only a lie, an empty talk? The poor in Britain are in dire need of welfare because, without it, around 1.3 million would fall into poverty. And his general response to it in private was: 'there's no magic money tree.' The other bad news is that he has plans for other rounds of austerity.

After twelve years in power, the Tories are almost out of ideas. It is evident from their systemic failures, as demand for food banks is outstripping supply, and social spending is drastically cut. At one point in time, Tories were known to have good political sense, with their cautious pragmatism and financial sobriety, which now it seems has all been eroded out. The Tories of today are synonymous with chaos, and it is leading to the ruination of Britain.

This decay made Peter Oborne write in New York Times: 'Like the Republicans in the United States, the Conservatives are detached from reality. In a generation, they have become a party of monomaniacs, incompetents, and ideologues. Like a thoroughbred that has run one race too many, it needs putting out to grass.'

October 31, 2022

47

AOUN'S HISTORIC MARITIME DEAL WITH ISRAEL

Israel and Lebanon are still technically at war, but an American-mediated deal for their maritime operations has been reached permanently. It aims to cease the future conflict. The deal was struck days before the Israeli election in October 2022. The debate regarding it had been highly politicised, with some questioning its motives and timing.

The deal was signed in restrained ceremonies in the respective countries. The occasion provided a rare occasion of harmony, but it also showed some limitations, as the Lebanese government believes that it is far less momentous than agreements reached between Israel and three Arab states in 2020, or Israel's earlier peace treaties with Egypt and Jordan. It signals that Lebanon is certainly a bit conservative and realistic about it. But, in Israel, the deal, in general, is regarded as a historic achievement that will bring prosperity, and stability, or as a fall of Hezbollah's threats, which fought wars with Israel in 2006, where fifteen hundred people were killed.

Before the deal, Hezbollah had vowed to cease any effort that seeks to drill an underwater gas field, Karish, near the disputed waters. In early 2022, Israel shot several drones that Hezbollah had sent, as a warning toward a rig at the Karish site, fuelling escalations.

After the deal, Hassan Nasrallah indicated in a press briefing that he was standing down on the gas issue.

One of its spokesmen revealed that they were no longer preparing for an imminent war. It was something that goes against their charter because it recognises Israel as an entity and not a state.

The maritime deal allocates drilling rights to Lebanon at one contested gas field, Qana, which straddles the two economic zones and confirms Israeli control of the Karish field on the Israeli side to the south.

Supporters of the deal argue that it removes the threat of immediate conflict with Hezbollah over the gas reserves. After the drafting, Lebanon could potentially reduce its dependence on Iranian oil as well.

For Sarit Zehavi, a former military officer in the intelligence corps described it as a deal yielding to the Lebanese position, asserting that it will postpone the next conflict. Amidror, a fellow of the conservative-leaning Jerusalem Institute for Strategy and Security and the Washington-based Jewish Institute for National Security of America has even concluded that the maritime deal would be good for Israel economically, but bad strategically.

Gas production has already begun from the Karish platform. Israel will also receive seventeen per cent of any future profits from the Lebanese Qana field, showing that Israel has an upper hand when it comes to boundaries. The royalties are to be paid by the French company prospecting there, as Lebanon rejected paying Israel directly.

'In addition to abandoning claims to Karish, Lebanon also seems to have dropped claims to a small safe zone that was owned and manned by Lebanese authorities,' claims Gulf News. It includes the area near the shore at Naqoura, extending around five kilometres out to the sea before it ties back to Line 23, which Israel has conceded to Lebanon.

In September 2022, however, Israel rejected the idea of a safe zone, ascertaining that it would put the northmost city of Nahariya at the mercy of Hezbollah fire. They suggested placing the would-be safe zone under the auspices of the United Nations, but that would require amending Unifil's current mandate, which applies to ground territory only and not to territorial waters.

The arrival of a new gas supply in the Mediterranean, nevertheless, is timely for Europe as it continues efforts to reduce its reliance on Russian supplies.

From the deal, Aoun also had certain things to prove. He wanted to show the regional politicians that he is a problem solver and that he was the man in charge of negotiations and not Parliament Speaker Nabih Berri, who had initiated talks over Lebanon's maritime borders in 2011. Aoun claimed that the talks fell under his authority, based on Article 52 of the Lebanese Constitution. Since then, however, he has found himself increasingly left out of the process, both by the Americans, Berri, and ironically, Hezbollah.

Aoun also wanted to have the final say on the disputed area, because it would have given him leverage with the US as he was trying to arrange the succession of his son-in-law and heir apparent, Gibran Bassil. Thus, he hopes that Bassil would succeed him as president when his term ends. That is why he tried trading the disputed territory in exchange for US endorsement for his son-in-law's presidential bid.

Before the deal, Netanyahu had criticised Lapid's decision for its affirmation. He accused him of spreading terrorism, and that the money generated from the deal would go to

Hezbollah's coffers. Lapid, in reply, called his comments 'irresponsible' and that talks with Lebanon have been 'very complex' until now.

November 28, 2022

48

LULA'S COMEBACK TO POWER IN BRAZIL

In Brazil, people believe that Lula has done a comeback of the century after winning the election. And he did that with a narrow margin and vowed to change the nation.

He had high approval ratings despite the notorious bribing charges in a vast corruption scheme in 2017. But this charge was refused by him and the Brazilian left. In 2021, Brazil's supreme court overturned his conviction, decreeing that his right to a free trial had been compromised. This cleared him to run for president again, where he campaigned around rebuilding public services, addressing inequality, and bringing down energy prices and inflation. He believed that his victory was nothing more than a referendum on democracy itself.

His win brings back to the fore a coalition of Brazil's large and disproportionately black class of the labouring poor who gave him the most support. It also included women who supported Lula's overwhelmingly amid a deeply patriarchal society and many progressive elements of the middle class. Lula promises to usher back in policies that favour moderate redistribution, a commitment to deepening social rights and environmental protection, including slowing the catastrophic destruction of Amazon. To many, he sounds like a typical nationalist, and not a neo-globalist, as some perceive him to be. He has also spoken the language of a liberal American or like a few European politicians who are against racism and democracy under siege. But hold on. It was Lula who constructed a hydroelectric dam in Amazon known as Belo Monte. That time, he had convinced the Xingu tribe that it was not the end of the world. So, when it comes to environmental protections on Amazon, he has fallen short of telling the global public the truth.

In his tenure, he will likely bring China and Russia closer to Brazil. However, he has challenging times ahead, as the Brazilian senate will be full of Bolsonaro's conservatives highlighting their agenda. The streets of Brazil may also become a crime pit again, as he was never hard on crime.

During Lula's tenure, it is hard to imagine how Americans maintained their relations with the Latin American country. It is because he forged alliances with Iran and Turkey to help Iran develop nuclear weapons, and recognised Palestine as a state, much to the discomfort of American eyes.

Despite the paradoxes and new developments that could take place, Lula's comeback to power has been ripe. As Bolsonaro captured international headlines, for dismantling environmental protections of the Amazonian rainforest, his fierce opposition to Covid-19 vaccines and social distancing, and a series of offensive statements about women, slum dwellers, and minorities, Lula got several political advantages ahead of him. But Bolsonaro had not accepted defeat initially, proclaiming at a rally that only God can remove him from office.

As a former military captain and an avowed supporter of military dictatorships, he wanted the military on his side to overturn the election result. After that, Bolsonaro told a justice on Brazil's supreme court that he wants to look ahead, and eventually accepted defeat.

In the beginning, he did not want to accept the election result because his campaign followers had claimed to have found a software bug in the voting machines, which would affect identification numbers. They believed that the bug would nullify about sixty per cent of votes in the machines, and had even filed a complaint for overturning the result.

By contrast before the result, Bolsonaro wanted the army to make a 'parallel vote count', according to The New York Times. The analysts also believe that military leaders are unlikely to support the coup at this tense time, even though Article 142 gives a kind of green pass for martial meddling in political affairs, no matter how much jurists bicker on its meaning.

As per reports by Time, the election day nevertheless was full of voter suppression aided by the military. In Lula's strongholds in the north and northeast, Brazil's federal police manned roadblocks. Locals also alleged a very high number of traffic stops for buses, disrupting travel to polling stations. In fact, during Bolsonaro's rule, the police director general Silviney Vasquez publicly supported Bolsonaro. A few months before the election, there were also around one hundred twenty-one politically motivated attacks recorded, including fifty-four murders.

Bolsonaro's loss also spoke of defeated American interventions in the name of Trump. As per an Op-ed in The New York Times by Natalia Vienna, Trump's political games were energetically adopted in Brazil by Bolsonaro. It is believed that Bolsonaro has been supported by influential figures in the American right, who were crucial to the Stop the Seal campaign.

As a former president, Bolsonaro spent intense time and

effort to build alliances in the United States, based on controversial far-right narratives, such as the threat of Communism and cultural Marxism. His son, Eduardo was named the South American representative of The Movement, and he also founded a conservative institute that helped organise the Brazilian version of the Pro-Trump Conservative Political Action Conference. That is where the contradictions concur because the subversion of democracy happening in Brazil in Bolsonaro's time would never have been allowed to have happened inside American democratic institutions. Thus, by being anti-American in support for their far-right policies in Brazil, Lula could try to sustain his rule.

December 2, 2022

49

ANWAR IBRAHIM'S CRACK AT POWER IN MALAYSIA

The new prime minister of Malaysia has been touted by some sections of the Malaysian and Western press as having the potential to usher Malaysia into a new direction. They believe that his election also gives a crucial chance for the nation to heal the social and political fabric, but the reality is that most of the notable leaders in Malaysia have not been clean slates. Even long-time serving prime minister, Najib Razak was indicted in 2022 for a twelve-year prison sentence for abuse of power, and money laundering related to 1MDB state fund. A US attorney general once described the embezzlement of billions of dollars from 1MDB as 'kleptocracy at its worst.'

Starting as a fiery student activist, and then becoming an establishment insider, Anwar was the man who took the country out of the Asian financial crises. He was perceived as a national leader since 1997 but was sacked by his nemesis turned mentor, Mahathir Mohammed a year later, for committing sodomy and corruptness, which he rebuffed as a political conspiracy. Ei Sun Oh from Singapore's Institute of International Affairs compares his political struggle with that of Nelson Mandela. Even Amnesty International called Anwar a 'prisoner of conscience.'

After the conviction was overturned, he returned to politics in 2004, as an opposition leader. But his future ambitions were dented by the second sentence for sodomy in 2015. After that, he ran from prison, in the 2018 election, re-joining Mahathir in a victorious new coalition. Eventually, a royal pardon let him resume political life after a nail-biting wait.

From 1998 and 2018, Anwar's popularity saw a steady decline, and the resurgent Umno, his ex-political party led by Razak, largely benefited from this. To some extent, it does speak of political survival but his moral compass also speaks of certain notoriety.

To up his local sentiment among the masses, he pledged to fight the rising cost of living, by saying that he will take no salary, but it all went in vain when he named the BN leader Ahmad Zahid Hamidi, as deputy prime minister, who faced graft charges. The hung parliament had made matters more complicated, as the king stepped in to choose the leader of the parliament who could form a cabinet.

What is even more concerning is the rise of the fundamentalist Malaysian Islamic Party (PAS) that won most seats in the 2022 election. Its ideology is fanatical to the extent that voting for other parties means going to hell, and political outsiders, including Malaysian Chinese, are viewed as infidels. In its strongholds of Kelantan and Terengganu, meat from cows, goats, and chickens slaughtered by Muslims who are not from their brethren is considered haram, thus creating an exclusionary 'us and them mentality' for the cause of implementing divine Shariah law. Many of the PAS-linked private Quran memorisation schools are set up by Malaysian students who returned home from the Middle East, particularly those from Jordan and Egypt. In urban centres, many Malay Muslims have become more religious, and many of them sign up for these schools, which are ubiquitous in urban areas, operating out of rented space in commercial buildings in city centres. Certain Muslim clerics believe that PAS has become intolerant under the leadership of current president Hadi, describing him as 'harsh' and 'dangerous,' after being 'accommodating' before. These developments will create more fissures in Anwar's rule, as rising fundamentalism will become a dangerous quandary for a multi-racial and multi-ethnic Malaysia.

When it comes to Anwar's cabinet, striking a balance between a representation of Malaysia's indigenous Malays and its ethnic Chinese and Indian minorities will be crucial, otherwise, he could find himself in further unsettling political trends. In foreign policy, he will most likely continue to foster equal ties with China, the US, Europe, and neighbours, which was an essence of the previous incumbent Najib Razak.

Anwar, unlike PAS leaders, is a strong proponent of mixing modern democracy with Islam, despite being a beneficiary of classical Western education. Enrolled at the University of Malaysia in Kuala Lumpur, he continued his advocacy for ethnic Malays, by creating several influential student organisations. It was during this time when he believed that Islam with modernism could be an emancipator for existing political and social problems, something that was common among many global Muslims, in the post-colonial period. That is why he also built connections with Muslims living abroad.

As some PH leaders, called the Alliance of Hope, resigned in 2020, Mahathir did not leave office as per his stated plan, which was to restate Anwar, by pardoning him and giving him a chance for re-election. Till 2022, PH remained in the opposition and eventually returned to power with Anwar as their leader. This scenario also reflects the love-hate relationship between Anwar and Mahathir at large.

The story of Anwar Ibrahim's success has even resonated with the Indonesians and the Filipinos, as they have reasons to be conscious about what is happening in Malaysia, despite their domestic issues of economic mismanagement and political despotism.

However, the most challenging thing to endure for Anwar would be that his cabinet will consist of his former foes. That is why making policies could become harder for him.

December 17, 2022

50

MARCOS FAMILY RULES PHILIPPINES AGAIN

It was being said that the 2022 presidential election win of Marcos Jr., son of former dictator Ferdinand Marcos Sr. was the most eventful since the 1986 People Power Revolution. It brought back dynastical democracy after the twenty-one-year rule of Marcos Sr., an era that was regarded in Philippine history as one of the darkest periods.

Historical memories were relived as another Marcos came into power. In the past, the Marcos family, known for its human rights abuses and corruption bankrupted the country and made it the 'sick man of Asia'. There was a systematic revisionist campaign orchestrated by Marcos's team, using different social media platforms.

These efforts, it was believed in the regional press, took more than a decade in making. After the election win, the political understandings of common Filipinos came to the fore.

According to an Op-ed by Michael Keel in Nikkei Asia: 'The Marcos family's return to the presidential palace in Manila is a window into a more disturbing world. It has laid bare pathologies that are rotting democracies in Asia and elsewhere from within. Many of these have roots in long-standing failures by elected governments to reduce social inequality and lift the living standards and dignity of poorer citizens. All this should make liberals reflect on the sense of renewed confidence they have displayed lately as powerful authoritarian states have stumbled.'

The 2022 election was also a replay of contests of other political dynasties. Sara Dutere, daughter of the outgoing president, Rodrigo Duterte tried to have her attempt at power, alongside Robredo from the reformist group. It is since 1992 when the Marcos family had made no secret plans to reclaim political power, and influence to re-establish the so-called Marcos legacy.

When it came to Marcos Jr., he had the advantage over Robredo as he had made a strategic partnership with Sara Duterte. It helped him strengthen his support base. However, he barely took part in debates and did not care about promoting unity. He even shrugged off previous convictions of tax evasion, as well as ongoing official efforts to recover the billions allegedly stolen during his father's rule. That is why the Philippines poll forms part of a contrasting narrative. In this story, more countries that conduct elections exhibit unplumbed regressive trends. It also shows a kind of generational failure in the modern democratic world.

Another characteristic feature of Marcos Jr.'s win was the outburst of misogyny his supporters directed at his liberal main opponent Robredo. Overt sexism has become increasingly prominent in mainstream political campaigning in democracies. It formed a strong current in Rodrigo Duterte's presidency, too.

When it came to Robredo, she relied more on grassroots support and volunteerism. While her campaign might have captured the hearts and minds of many of her supporters, who came in droves in her 'pink rallies,' organised mainly by young people, it drew comparisons to the 'yellow rallies' back then in 1986. However, the immensity and the reach of Marcos-Duterte resources dwarfed them. That is why

Marcos's victory was expected. And, according to him, he wants to bring the good old days of the old Marcos regime, which according to his revisionist campaign was prosperous and stable.

Although, there is a concern in the certain quarter of the Philippines policy community, as they think there is a lack of clarity in his platform. They are concerned about how he will address the immense challenges the Philippines is facing, especially when his family history speaks of cronyism, repression, and kleptocracy. With Sara Duterte as vice president, Marcos Jr. will likely protect his predecessor from investigations, and possible prosecution for human rights violations and extrajudicial killings carried out during his war on drugs policy.

In the Philippines, there are growing food crises, water and resource scarcity, growing energy demands, and the urgent need to marshal the impact of climate change. The December 2022 protests regarding his rule already speak of an abandoned situation.

In terms of foreign policy, the Philippines must address the growing need for relations with the United States, China, and its ASEAN neighbours. But, foreign policy, surprisingly, has been absent from the campaign of Marcos Jr.

One of the most pressing issues for the Philippines is the future of the West Philippine Sea. The outgoing Duterte administration has taken a non-confrontational approach toward China and adopted almost a fatalistic attitude on the West Philippine Sea issue. Under Duterte, the Philippines leaned more towards trade and investment with Beijing.

Marcos Jr. is expected to continue Duterte's friendly

policy with China. But he must make sure that the Philippines does not see itself getting in between the US-China competition. According to an article by Jonathan Stromseth in Brookings Institution, this will bring into question how Marcos Jr. would deal with the United States and the future of the US-Philippines alliance. During the old Marcos regime, the military partnership remained resilient, despite the US opposition to martial law, reflecting the double games and lip service of liberty by Americans. The outgoing president had a grudge towards the United States, but Marcos Jr. has no known personal baggage.

Given Marcos Jr.'s cosmopolitan background, he is perhaps less insular and more inclined to pursue relations with the United States than with China, and in his tenure, will likely adopt a neutral position when it comes to US-China rivalry. More ever, Filipinos have a more favourable view of the United States than China. Given the kind of economic and transnational issues, the Philippines is facing, it will be important to ponder whether Marcos will support multilateralism regionally and globally.

December 19, 2022